Herding Does Not Make You Happy

Harry Noad

Copyright © 2013 Harry Noad

All rights reserved.

ISBN: 1490979778

ISBN-13: 978-1490979779

For Mike. God only knows what I'd be without you.

CONTENTS

Introduction	6
Aims	10
Peer Pressure	17
Clothes	23
Friends	29
Parties	36
Drugs	41
Sex	48
Work	54
Hobbies	60
Ambition	66
Reading	71
Words	76
Parents	81
Money	87
Music	93

Relationships	99
Honesty	105
Adversity	111
Gossip	117
Travel	123
Food	128
Patriotism	134
Change	139
Unfairness	144
Death	149
Bravery	152
Sacrifice	157
Conversation	162
Slowing Down	167
Hope	171
The End	177

ACKNOWLEDGMENTS

I would like to thank everyone who has encouraged and supported me through the process of writing my first book; especially my mother, my excellent editor Zander Sharp and the teachers at Hurstpierpoint College who inspired me and always encouraged me to be true to myself rather than "one of the unthinking herd."

Harry Noad is currently studying Philosophy and Theology at St Peter's College, Oxford. He wrote this book over the course of his final year at school.

EPIGRAPH

'Man cannot remake himself without suffering, for he is both the marble and the sculptor.'

Alexis Carrel

PREFACE

Aristotle once said that we are what we repeatedly do. He followed this up with a statement on excellence and how it was therefore not an act, but a habit. I believe the mantra is much more resonant when we realise that if all we ever do is squander our personality for the sake of others, we become little more than a shell. A hollow impression of a human, duty-bound to make others like us at the expense of anything and everything that makes us like ourselves. If we live for others, we do not live at all, and it startles me to think that for years I lived in the shadow of my enemies, contemporaries, and even my friends. I wasn't happy, but it was the only way I knew. For many years I was trapped in perpetual negativity, until one day something snapped.

An epiphany. For the first time, I could see that real change was a possibility (a necessity, even) in my life and that I didn't have to waste another minute pandering to people I didn't even like. Over the next few months I grew happier by the day as I began dressing, acting and talking the way I wanted to, unencumbered by the pressures of teenage society. Years flew by as I blossomed into the person I always knew I could be. The day I let go was the best day of my life.

Of course, that was only the beginning. The route to true change is a long and treacherous one, and I've encountered serious hardship along the way. It's a challenging prospect, and my dream is to help others on their journey any way I can. This book is the fruit of that dream, and it's been a long time coming. I was positive that it should be written by a teenager for a young audience, whilst the experiences that shaped me remained fresh in my mind. As a result, every spare moment of my last year at school was spent on this book. When I wasn't revising, I went back and modified chapters, trying to write something that I hoped would change people's lives one day.

Soon, however, everything stalled. I had a busy summer, and the book was firmly on the back burner. Preparations for University struck me as the bigger fish to fry, and so the book remained a messy word document on my computer. Sadly, it took real tragedy to shake me from my stupor and encourage me to finish what I had started. I had begun to think of the book as merely a pastime that I had evolved beyond, but the untimely passing of a close friend reminded me of life's brevity. I needed to spread my message, and if I could help just one person doing it then I'd be happy.

Before long it was finished. I sat with more than a year's work in front of me and felt that familiar, overwhelming urge returning to me. It wasn't enough to have written all of this down, it needed to be spread, and fast. This book was a catalogue of my experiences bound together by advice and suggestions. I thought of young people freeing themselves from the constraints of peer pressure and societal influence and felt happy, confident that my book could help them achieve this goal.

The themes are multitudinous and range from the arguably trivial to the unarguably significant. I wanted this book to be helpful whether your issue was with the shoes you wore or the death of a relative, and I hope that shines through. Some of the chapters reflect my unfortunate lack of life experience, but I hope that the design of them enables them to be used as a guide rather than an instruction - in most cases anyway. Like everyone else, I've only lived one life, and I've been extremely fortunate with the hand I've been dealt. Nevertheless, I feel that this book addresses issues that are relevant to young people everywhere, and not just those who share my race, gender, financial status or religious viewpoint.

It's of paramount importance to me that the book isn't perceived as being patronising or condescending and I've tried hard to show that through my writing. I want it to be accessible to anybody and everybody who wants to read it and gain something from it. I struggled with chapters such as 'Parents' since my family is all anybody could ever ask for, and my parents two of the most wonderful people I've ever met. Of course, they aren't without their flaws, but my home life was certainly more stable than most. It took some stern words from my editor and good friend to make me think more deeply about what I'd written and try to reach a wider audience. The same can be said for chapters referencing drug use, something of which I have no experience at all. All things considered, I tried my best to adopt a standpoint of neutrality, and apologise for instances where my personal opinion intruded unwelcomingly. Efforts were made to keep them to a minimum.

The book is designed to be read chronologically, though in truth it's just as easy to drop in on any chapter after the first couple if and when it's applicable to events unfolding in a reader's life. Each section is aptly labelled and condensed into an easily digestible length. A much-needed edit helped cut out some of the less essential chapters, resulting in a refined product that is not watered-down so much as intensely concentrated.

On the subject of my editor, Zander Sharp, I cannot thank him enough. A brighter student and more rounded individual I have yet to meet, and I feel that he's the model that I and anybody who reads this book should aspire to. His home life may not have been perfect, but he's come out of it a confident, charismatic and kind individual. Through no small toil he's made himself into a better person and thrown off the shackles of expectation and pressure to make himself the very best 'him' he could ever have been. What's more, he was unerringly ruthless in his edit, and the end product that you hold in your hands owes as much to him as it does to me. The world needs more people like him: he certainly isn't part of the herd.

We are what we repeatedly do. So read on. Make changes and stick to them. Be fiercely committed to your cause, and don't give it up for anybody. Strive to come ever-closer to perfection and prepare to become what you always knew you could be… yourself.

Chapter 1: INTRODUCTION

'The beginnings of all things are small'

-Cicero

The past is a big place. Sometimes, it's a horrible place. Nobody's in love with their past, and I don't know anybody who wants to remember everything they've ever done. Nobody's lived a perfect existence, and there are always going to be occurrences - people, places, actions – that we choose to forget. At the same time, however, there are things that happen that we'll want to remember for the rest of our lives; instances when we wish time would halt and we could exist – unencumbered by age and hardship – forever. We wish that everyone would stay the same, and we resent them when they change. We cling to tradition but spend all day discussing how to make the world better. We convince ourselves that we, as human beings, are the pinnacle of evolution. The be-all and end-all. We've come so far in our brief existence, conquered this world entire. Who's to say we won't go further? What's the limit of mankind? My aim with this book is to prove that it's worth letting go of the past to increase your chances of monumentally altering your own life, taking stock of the current situation and improving it to forge for yourself a new and beautiful existence. Of course, there are memories that can and should be preserved eternally, but gripping too tightly to everything that holds us back is what prevents us as individuals from viewing ourselves as truly exceptional.

There are plenty of big questions already flying about, but the answers aren't all we want them to be. People change, age affects us all, nobody dies entirely satisfied. It's hard to wrap your head round the fact that life isn't infinite. People tell me that once you approach the dark embrace of death you take one of two routes. There's the first, where you welcome your fate with open arms, and walk hand in hand with the reaper towards your inevitable destiny. That, or you fight tooth and nail to cling to this life as long as you can. The second pathway doesn't sound nearly as fun. One of the saddest things to happen to a person is to reach death without ever having lived. Sadder still is the fact that most of us only realise this once it's too late. Deathbed disciples either looking up expectantly, or glancing over their shoulder to ensure they've still got enough time to make things work. Looking back to see Father Time grinning back at them. Personally, I'd rather be greeting my destruction content in the knowledge that I'd done everything I possibly could to lead a worthwhile life.

It's always interesting to think about how fragile we can be. I mean, a fact I always wheel out is that it only takes fifteen pounds of force to collapse the trachea. If it's that easy to completely cripple someone then I can't help but question the big man upstairs. I'm not trying to paint myself as omniscient here, but surely the appendix was either a massive design flaw or a horribly dark joke. Far from oesophageal weakness, it's even easier to take our metaphorical breath away. Even if we haven't all pondered the inadequacy of the human frame, we've all been witness to our own mental inadequacy. In the world we live in today, depression is omnipresent, and there are plenty of people struggling on a daily basis to combat their own personal demons. On a completely unrelated note, too many of us are too caught up in our own neuroses to realise when somebody really needs us. We've been raised to look out for number one, and programmed to put our own interests first. Whilst I still think that's the ultimate aim, the fact is sometimes other people need you a hell of a lot more than you need yourself.

It's interesting to consider where we'd be if we had or hadn't made the decisions we made or didn't make. The fact is, we'll never be able to go back and change anything about our past. Sometimes that fact is hard to take, but it's of central importance that we acknowledge and accept it. The past is just that: passed. We can't go back and rectify a poor decision any more than we can go back and stop Stalin or Hitler, prior to their malevolent actions. I suppose it may be apt to funnel this into the mould of a lesson; the first of many. The sooner we can learn to accept the fact that our lives have a clearly defined beginning, middle and end, the sooner we can learn to enjoy every minute of it. Time is a constant. And every journey starts somewhere.

Chapter 2: AIMS

'The bud may have a bitter taste, but sweet will be the flower'

– Cowper

It's such a cliché to start off by talking about where things started. All the conventional writers start off by beginning at the beginning. But that isn't what this story is about. This isn't a story about how love is horrible, or not real, or how I've suffered. It's not even a story about how I started my school life as a boy and left as a man. It's not a novel, or a self-help guide, or a monologue. Think of this as an autobiography, written by someone who isn't rich or famous enough to have a ghost writer to write one for him. And the point of it? Essentially, I'm setting out to make people feel good about themselves. This isn't a plaster over a wound that needs stiches, either. If you sit down to read this book, I hope you'll stick around for the long haul. Improving your existence takes time, commitment and a whole lot of effort. In that respect, I guess, you could call this a guide to making yourself a better person, but who really needs ill-defined labels like 'better' anyway? I just want to help those looking for change to find it. The introductory ramble was there to root out the active from the passive, the bold from the timid. Let's be honest with ourselves here, if you weren't able to wade through seven-hundred words of juvenile psychobabble, how are you going to keep focus for another few hundred pages?

I'm just like you. Whoever you are, wherever you are, if you're reading this it means we're kindred spirits. I'm no aged University professor speaking from an untold treasure trove of life experience, I'm just a teenager who cocked his head one day and started to look at my world with a different pair of eyes. It's important for me that everyone connects with the author as much as the book - I see these pages as a conduit through which I can reach you, on the other side. Remember as you work your way through this (if you ever manage to get to the other side) that I'm no guru. You're the real leader in this party; I'm just here for the atmosphere.

Don't worry; the fact that you've made it this far is positive, it shows you're at least slightly intrigued by the premise of this work and open to the possibility of making a change. As I said before, it isn't going to be a walk in the park, but with a little grit and determination it will happen. If you've got the guts to read, I've got the tale to tell. Again, it's clichéd to argue that I represent a minority, but I feel that that word is the only one yet invented to describe my constituency, and by that I mean the scores of intellectual, over-analytical men and women who aren't comfortable taking the world at first glance; Those people who question the nature of society along with the legitimacy of authority. No, not the big-headed, small-minded bugbear brigade who will complain about anything with the word 'party' at the end of it. The people that I refer to are merely questioners. They aren't content to coast through life, rolling with the punches and simply accepting the way the world is. If something's right, then they'll leave it be. If something isn't right, they'll harbour a deep-seated resentment, whether or not they have the power or impetus to try and rectify the problem. A whole generation of people willing to buck the trend, to change something for themselves rather than wallowing in self-pity. Maybe you're one of the people still stuck in the 'mope' stage, in which case I envy you somewhat. You're about to experience one of the greatest moments of your life. Personally, I can safely say that my own 'epiphany' (for lack of a better word) was probably the turning point of my life so far.

But that is an experience that we have yet to address. I feel that before anybody can get anywhere near such a radical change, it's important to lay the foundations, to put in the groundwork. Rome wasn't built in a day, and a new existence sure isn't either. There isn't really a concrete place to start, because everyone's journey is bound to be different and unique. Something which is universal is this moment: this is the beginning; the beginning of change. There's no way we can change ourselves before we learn to accept and transcend the limitations of the person that we are. So, here we have it, the initial stair, plain and simple. Religious types could jot this down as the first step towards enlightenment. I don't feel it's a generalisation to claim that everyone has to pass through each of these stages to reach their goal, and it strikes me as self-evident that putting in the work for getting over the hump of your early enlightenment is what makes the rest feel all the better. Once you've climbed the hill, you're all the more excited to begin skipping down the other side.

There's something that I distinctly recall experiencing that I'm certain wasn't exclusive to me. I remember feeling stuck between my own desires and what everybody else wanted me to be, and feeling completely at odds with two different sides of myself. This is the desperate struggle to identify with the in-crowd, to be a part of something larger than yourself. Anything before this is irrelevant. Growing up has nothing on growing out. People get stuck in this regrettable stage for their whole lives, hating what they've become and yet never doing anything about it. For some, this is inevitable. They either have the wrong approach, or the wrong attitude. These are the people most deserving of our sympathy. I learned a long time ago that hating people doesn't get you anywhere. I'm fully aware of how superbly affable this may make me seem, but the real route of this 'kindliness' is that hating people merely gives other people a reason to hate you. Be honest with yourself and think about the amount of hate already in your daily life, do we really need any more petty arguments? I don't think so. Maybe compassion is the road to go down with these people. It allows you to feel comfortable offering them small kindnesses, and each one of them will make you feel like a better person. Of course, good intentions are important here, and nobody ever improved their lives by taking the easy road. It takes a whole lot of sweat and tears, and an unwavering command of your deepest impulses. Revenge may be sweet, but rising above such insignificant trifles tastes all the sweeter, and the respect you'll garner for being such a down-to-earth person is like a cool glass of lemonade on a hot afternoon.

I digress. I should talk more about the trap of identification; the pitfall that claims so many young and impressionable souls. In fact, rather than a trap, think of it as something of a rite of passage. Something that everyone has had to traipse down at least once in their life. Envisage a set of hot coals which you have to walk through. No shoes, no socks, no salve. Just get down to it and walk. You cringe; you go right back to square one. Only those who push their way through to the other side get to move on. Eventually, your soles will harden, and your feet will get used to it. You'll convince yourself that life on the lava isn't so bad. But there's that niggling thought, that little insect that you just can't swat. The feeling that there's more to life than strong feet, and the ability to withstand hardship. The idea that there are more reasons to cross the road than simply to get to the other side.

Chapter 3: PEER PRESSURE

'Of all beasts the man-beast is the worst; to others and himself the cruellest foe'

– R. Baxter

People spend their whole lives stuck in one place. Always keeping up with the neighbours, but never being the one that people are trying to keep up with. Some people will do anything to be cool, and here I feel a personal anecdote (if it can really be called that) feels relevant.

Part one: Sad. I had an acquaintance once, someone in the same year as me at school. We were all at the prime age to fall victim to the predatory misery moguls that are poised to swoop on anybody. That is, as long as it gets the insecurity of their own status off their minds. Deflection is paramount for these vultures: shift the blame, pass the torch. The sad truth is they're all exactly the same. There is no kingpin, no head honcho. Everybody acts the way they act out of fear that the rest of the group will vilify them if they act any different. But anyway, back to the acquaintance. I think we'll keep him an anonymous hero, because I know some of you are going to identify with this fable and I feel he deserves to remain nameless. He's just a young boy who wants to be part of the in-crowd. Who doesn't, right? Well, soon this boy is going to find out in an all-too real way that once you commit yourself to joining the group, it's hard to stop yourself from sliding all the way down the slippery slope. It begins with light mockery, and our 'hero' is willing to cut these guys a little slack if it'll get his feet off the ground and help him gain a foothold – anything – in this Shangri-La: the cool group.

It worsens, of course, as time goes by. He inexplicably acquires a nickname: 'faggot'. To any well-adjusted human being this stopped being funny a while ago, and is a pejorative insult that we wouldn't choose to use. Frankly, it's offensive, and about as far from humour as a nickname can get. For an immature group of teenage boys, it's hilarious. To see someone fully accept it as their nickname, blissfully ignorant of the ulterior motives of the group behind branding this poor bastard with a nickname he'll never shake, is really sad. Anyway, things change, the group evolves, he keeps getting picked on. Gossip flows, and we come to hear a little more about this guy. Seems that over the past few months he's been slowly eking his way into the group, or so he thought. In reality, it was the desire of the other kids to exploit his resources that meant they kept him around. More time passes, he gets used a little more, he's pretty much 'their faggot' now. He willingly hangs out with this group – that much is vital to remember. Nobody forces him except the cold hands of peer pressure, societal pressure, parental, even: to be cool. He's necking shots like nobody's business at parties because he's convinced it will make him cool.

Part two: Sadder. A few of the kids go over to his house one day to play games, because he's 'loaded' enough to have the newest consoles and whatnot. Obviously, these kids have some supernatural power to locate alcohol and at their age it's the most exciting thing ever. Of course, being cool, they can't show this, so they just find a way into the parent's liquor cabinet and have at it. People are pulling down curtains, drawing on photos on the walls, it's chaos. I remember my informant getting very animated when talking about one particular guy hell-bent on leaving a nice arse-print in the parents' swanky glass table, and managing to crack it right down the middle.

The worst part is one of them kicking his dog – a cute little golden retriever, I'd seen his Dad out walking it before – and our man just standing by and laughing. It's almost enough to make you hate the guy, and you would, if you didn't understand just how much he hated himself already.

Part three: Saddest. His Dad came home, to find the whiskey bottles strewn about the place, and his home in a sorry state. Understandably upset, he tells the kid to explain himself, shell-shocked somewhat at the mishmash of broken glass and vandalised memorabilia in which he finds himself. The rowdy boys don't even bother to quieten down, keeping their rambunctious activity with no signs of stopping. One of them cries out 'Fuck off, Faggot Senior' to whoops of laughter from his lackeys. Immediately, the kid himself regales his own father with 'Yeah, shut up, Faggot Senior!'.

Nobody laughs. His Dad looks at him with the most sincere pity imaginable in his eyes, and begins to pick up the broken glass. The rest of the kids go back to heckling and general misbehaviour, and boy wonder shrugs off his faux pas with reckless abandon. I saw the kid again a few years ago, and he's tripled in size and has been diagnosed with schizophrenia after his cocaine use.

Miserable. I know some readers will reach this point of the chapter with a wry smile on their faces, confident that the kid got his comeuppance in the end. But you're missing the point entirely. That poor guy should evoke no emotion but sadness and compassion. If you want to be happy with yourself, you have to stop wishing bad things on other people. Anger will only lead to unhappiness, vengeance to more anger. A vicious circle indeed. I feel sorry for his Dad, I feel sorry for the hours he must have spent picking up broken glass, and I really feel for that poor puppy. But nobody deserves more sympathy than these people. Sympathy for those who haven't had the opportunity or incentive to push past this stage of their own personal development is so important, because it helps us become happy, well-rounded people in our own right. Concerning ourselves with the issues that others face helps us to get some perspective on issues that may be troubling ourselves, which in turn can lead to a happier all-round existence. For this particular case, it would appear that a significant number of issues need addressing.

It's important to realise where this kid really went wrong. It wasn't with his friends, his attitude or even with his father. It sounds clichéd to say that the person who the kid betrayed the most was himself, because he let himself get sucked under by the integration undercurrent, but it's true. He wasn't strong enough to swim against the flow, and so he ended up drowned by his own inability to fight for a cause he felt was important to him. I think we could assume that he didn't talk smack to his Dad of his own inspiration, so where did he go wrong? Before we answer that question, I think it could be beneficial to talk about a really easy way to make yourself feel better in the short term and help yourself establish some sort of long term locus of control because, let's be honest, if you can't pick out your own clothes, your life needs a serious adjustment!

Chapter 4: CLOTHES

'Clothes make the man. Naked people have little or no influence on society'

– Mark Twain

The irony of labels like 'Independent' and 'Alternative' never ceases to amuse and exasperate in equal measure when you realise how inaccurate they are. It's an-all too common occurrence to witness a gang of friends wandering around a shopping centre, looking like they've just walked out of an Abercrombie catalogue. Of course, this is true of those who try even harder to stray from the masses, too. People who ironically wear clothes traditionally viewed as vomit-inducingly 'uncool' for the sole reason of being different, rather than because they genuinely like what they're wearing, are no less a slave to the system than those who do conform. Similarly, I don't feel compelled to completely push the boat out with colour or style, but that's a personal choice. When people describe me by saying I wear 'off-the-wall' I don't think they mean on-the-ceiling. I found what works for me, so find what works for you; if that's an all-brown ensemble then go with it, make it your own and enjoy it for what it is. Just because someone else enjoys wearing their own rainbow braces doesn't mean that they're the be-all-and-end-all when it comes to clothing. What really matters is your own taste and opinion. The key to escaping this particular loop is so simple, and yet eludes so many people. Cliché number one: be yourself.

What I mean by 'yourself' may not be immediately obvious. I don't believe it is to anybody. It takes a lot of experimentation and exasperation before we discover what we really are. Even today I know fewer people that know themselves than I do people who only seem to know illusions of themselves. A lot fewer. It takes a lot of experimentation, and it's very important here to discover a style that you feel you belong to, whatever that may be. You like wearing woolly hats with t-shirts? You wear woolly hats and t-shirts. You like wearing a crown on a daily basis? Feel free. You like wearing pink and yellow striped romper suits? Do so. It really doesn't matter what it is, as long as it's what you really want. There isn't any point in convincing yourself that you really do like something, either, if your reasoning is flawed. If you tell yourself enough times that snapbacks are what you really love wearing, especially if they still have the labels on, then you'll believe it yourself, even if it isn't what you really feel deep down. I started out with pink shoelaces, because they fit with the shoes I had at the time and I liked having unconventional colours in my clothing. It doesn't matter what it is, and I can't stress that point enough. There's nothing worse than the feeling of being so utterly conformist that the only thing keeping you out of an Abercrombie catalogue is your dangerously low sense of self-confidence. Of course, the message that I transmitted before still stands, and if you genuinely like the feeling of having just stepped out of a catalogue then by all means, wear that gear and enjoy it. Don't let me tell you that it's the wrong thing to wear if you really feel comfortable and happy in it.

This kind of thinking is crucial to feeling good about yourself. One of the most important mantras to live by is something so simple: know thyself. If this book was like other books, then I'd use this chapter as the first one, because clothes are, in essence, the beginning of the new person you'd like to be. Over time, your own personal style with evolve and flourish, but everybody has to start somewhere. Presumably, most of those reading this book will be or formerly have been unhappy, to some degree. A brand new wardrobe can go so far in fixing this. People aren't telling the whole truth when they say that clothes don't matter, because while what you're wearing itself doesn't matter, the symbolism inherent within your attire has a deep and personal meaning to you. If it doesn't, it should do. It's amazing the compliments people afford those individuals who are ready and willing to be their own person and step out of line, ever so slightly, with regards to dress.

Hair is another gold mine of creative potential: male or female, school or college rules notwithstanding, your hairstyle can come to illustrate the image of yourself you want to project to all others. Personally, as of a few weeks ago I favour the shaved-all-over look, but it's so much fun to experiment and discover a stylistic direction that feels right to you. Once you set off, you'll find it hard to stop, and a train of this size in motion is very hard to halt once it builds up a full head of steam. It doesn't even have to stop there, you can start editing your shoes, socks, underpants, whatever, all of it contributes to turning yourself into your own person, rather than a cardboard cut-out. Every time I go out I feel comfortable and confident, two words which are going to become absolutely key as this education unfurls. So next time you're tempted to pick up something that you know is fashionable for that reason alone, maybe try it on in the dressing room, have a walk around the shop and ask yourself who you're really buying it for. If it isn't you, then who's it for? And why aren't they in the shop, sitting on one of those god-awful leather seats and demanding that you try it in the next size up?

The key point here is that this clothing issue is simply another ace in the pack for conformity, as if everybody looks exactly the same, there's no basis for rebellion or individuality. If you feel strongly enough about something, you're only letting yourself down if you don't pursue it with everything you have. It's a proven psychological fact that it only takes a single follower to do something before everyone breaks away and joins it. 'But', I hear you cry, 'we have nobody to follow!' Here lies the greatest gift you have: the potential to be a forerunner, to lay a path anew for those wonderful people who lock away their flares and rainbow braces for fear of ridicule. If you don't want that, then just be satisfied to coast along, happy and content in the knowledge that you're wearing your clothes, and you're rocking them. It's a wonderful feeling to help people express themselves, knowing that you once stood at the same precipice of individuality they find themselves on. Being different helps other people be different, and being yourself helps others find who they want to be. The excellent Theophilus London once said that 'the clothes don't make the man, it's the man that makes the clothes', so you wear your pink shoelaces to school, and you wear them with pride.

Chapter 5: FRIENDS

'True friends stab you in the front'

- Wilde

One of the most important parts of feeling good is surrounding yourself with people who make you feel good. The power of a collective behind you that supports the choices you make whilst still standing up to you with your best interests at heart should never be underestimated. What's most vital here is to distinguish between your friends and those who pretend to be close to you for their own personal gain. In the story of 'Faggot' a few chapters back we saw how easy it is to get sucked into the trap of supplying everything whilst receiving nothing. I hasten to add, this is not to say that you should rely on those around you to supply you with a constant stream of things that make you happy. That's not what friends are for. Your friends are there to keep you grounded, to be there for you when you have a problem and to help you realise when you're going wrong. This project of making yourself happy is never an easy one, and it is inevitably accompanied by lapses of confidence. In instances such as this you need your friends to scrape you off the pavement, put you on your feet again, brush you down and send you off to give it another shot. Without them, you're just an insecure mess stuck to the cement.

This may sound like a selfish interpretation of what it is to be involved in a friendship, and it's true that friendship is a two-way street. Where the selfishness comes in is in learning to enjoy every aspect of each friendship you establish. Helping one of your friends overcome something that's bothering them should give you every bit as much pleasure as you gain from their assistance. It's important here to note that someone that you share mutual aid with is not necessarily your friend. If you're merely helping each other out with problems you can't fix by yourself, then they aren't your friend. Friendship requires a deep commitment from you both. If there is an excess or deficiency of commitment from either side of the friendship fence, the connection won't blossom and you'll be left exactly where you started: two strangers who happened to need problems solved at the same time.

Friends can come from anywhere. There is no mould of what a friend should be, and you can be friends with anybody, as long as you care about each other enough to put yourselves through the toils of becoming close in the first place. It's never easy to construct a friendship from nothing with somebody, but in my experience a good first step is to go up to somebody and strike up a conversation with them. Most people (at least the ones you'd want to be friends with!) won't reject your advances and will probably be quite impressed that you had the balls to come and talk to them. It's funny that this is the first time confidence is being seriously referenced, because it's really the crux of everything that is going to make you happy in this world. If you can manage to push past the trials and tribulations that come with making friends, dressing how you want, building your own identity and making yourself happy, the benefits will show themselves in no time. With friends in particular, a certain degree of confidence, without overshooting into arrogance territory, is something that can ensure you maintain the friendships you have and, as you do so, gain an idea of how to branch out to reach more people. If you have the confidence to go up to somebody that you'd previously had down as something of a social outcast, you could chance upon a plethora of interesting people that had been hiding right under your nose whilst you were too busy looking elsewhere. Some people can be so fantastic to have around given half a chance. If you try your hardest to integrate yourself into a group and they still don't fancy having you around, then move on. One of the best pieces of advice I've ever received is that being rejected doesn't matter, and that there are literally billions of people just waiting to be met and greeted.

It's important to see the good in everybody. There is nobody that should be ruled out as a potential friend, simply because nobody is really 'beyond help'. Everyone starts in the same place; nobody is born a better person than anybody else. We are what we make ourselves. If we simply stopped and thought for a little while every day, we could make ourselves into much better, more well-rounded and inherently happier people. The way to start making people think this way is to reach out to them. Everybody is capable of improvement, simply because nobody is perfect. Similarly, nobody is fully imperfect. Everyone has something about them that is a wonderful thing. Gangs of bullies often show evidence of extreme loyalty to their fellows. 'Honour' is a word I hear bandied around often in reference to those who obsess over vengeance and comeuppance, often with violent results. The key is isolating these positive elements in people and doing all that is within your power to make people better. You improve yourself by improving others. A happy existence is one in which you are surrounded by people you've helped that are prepared to help you with any problem you could have. There's no threat of animosity between true friends, as they will come through any struggle with their bond even stronger at the end. Your wolf pack has to reflect the values that you yourself hold. Surround yourself with open-minded people, and you'll be well on your way to achieving everything that you want to. A friend will be there to pat you on the back when you succeed and scold you readily when you fail. If you can reach this level of commitment with somebody, they'll stick by you through thick and thin. The problem is all of this requires significant effort from you. No resting on your laurels here: if you want true friends, you're going to have to work for them, and work with them.

Make time for people. If somebody has a problem, drop what you're doing to help them out. This builds trust, which is a cornerstone of a successful friendship. If one of your friends invites you out then they want to spend time with you. Go out with them, if only to make them happy. Who knows, something that sounds dire on the invite can often turn out strangely enjoyable if you give it half a chance and the right people are attending. Feel free around your friends to become the person you want to be. If you expect honesty from them, then be frank with them. Pull no punches in telling a friend how you feel towards them or their actions. Snidely remarking on so-and-so's lack of deodorant usage helps nobody, least of all you. Don't gossip in your friendship groups, talk about something that matters. Not every chat has to be Mariana trench deep, but try and maintain some level of sophistication in what you're saying to each other. People get bored easily of boring conversation. However, it's true that on occasion everybody needs to cut loose and let their hair down when it comes to idle chatter. Sometimes it has to be just that: idle. Some of the funniest moments I have with my friends aren't sophisticated in the slightest, but they're hilarious because they embody our friendship so precisely that it doesn't even matter that they are, in essence, the height of bad taste. Nobody wants to eat conversational caviar every day, so what's wrong with a bit of burger banter every now and then?

Use your friends as springboards to do what you want, and be there for them when they have their own ambitions. Most importantly, work together to pick each other up when you're down. You may be able to function without your friends when you're having a good time, but when depression's knocking at your door there's nobody you value more. True friends are like umbrellas. Sharp, always there for you, with more beneath the surface than it seems. And they'll always be able to comfort you when the rain comes down.

Chapter 6: PARTIES

'Ever notice that Soup for One is eight aisles away from Party Mix?'

– Elayne Booster

Every once in a while everybody, without exception, finds themselves feeling uncomfortable on a night out. Be it a house party or an evening spent gallivanting with girls that would look more at home in an Ann Summers catalogue than a moderately priced drink/dance venue (e.g. clubbing), nobody is immune from social awkwardness. Even those who appear the most confident at first glance are prone to the occasional lapse in machismo, leading to the inevitable huddles of similarly minded folk that litter the 'party scene' these days. The key here is to not get sucked in to a situation in which you'll be trapped in the same place for the entire night, hanging out with the same people you spend every day with at school, college, University, whatever. A night out is THE prime opportunity to meet new people, and if your school is anything like mine, this chance is a godsend. These people could develop into your very closest friends and if you lock yourself into your small, safe little group then you could never meet any of them. Let's be honest, what have you got to lose by chatting to a couple of strangers? Worst case scenario is they offer you a half-hearted reply and leave you alone to get on with having fun. Never concern yourself with what other people think of you in times like these, and just do whatever it takes to overcome the awkwardness that walks hand in hand with the first few hours of any modern get-together. If that means finding a little Dutch courage just to grease the wheels, so be it. Whatever it takes (within reason, watch those shots) to give you the impetus to approach people, do it. Strap on a metaphorical pair and talk to these people.

The conversation itself doesn't even have to be anything special. As I mentioned before, a lot of people are impressed by you coming to talk to them in the first place, and taking an interest in somebody can only ever lead to a hearty conversation on their part, without you having to even say anything most of the time. Alcohol, again, can be your friend here, as people loosen up considerably once they've knocked a couple back, and it's entirely possible to maintain a conversation of any description with someone just by asking them questions and responding appropriately. If you're not the chatting type, there's always the dancefloor. Too many people get embarrassed when they dance, or try to. Once again, your confidence is all that matters here. You could be throwing yourself around like a ragdoll on Ritalin and people will love you for it, simply because you've got the balls to do it. More importantly, you'll feel good. There's a real sense of relief once you realise that you don't have shackles round your ankles, and that you'll actually look more of a joke if you stand in the corner awkwardly rather than actually going for it, throwing a couple of shapes, making yourself look a fool but loving every second of it. The devil-may-care attitude is infectious, and it only takes you being strong enough to laugh at yourself to encourage all those around you to consider chancing whatever deluded reputations they have (seriously, did all these people go to dance college or something? Why do people care so much about how they look when everybody's wasted anyway?) and bust a move alongside you.

The other advantage to simply throwing caution to the wind and getting jiggy with it, be it in conversational or literal format, is that people will find you a lot more interesting, and everybody wants to be friends with the interesting guy. If you combine acting like you don't care what anybody says about you with dressing like you don't care what anybody says about you, then you're on the right path. If you pull it off, by which I mean NEVER giving up and resorting to dressing for anybody else, or leaving the dancing brigade because someone flashes you a look of disgust, then you're laughing. You get to wear what you want, act how you want, and gain a huge amount of respect whilst doing it. Be confident in your actions, your outfit, and most of all your choice of words. Don't beat around the bush with anyone you meet, or try to embellish anything about you. A little light exaggeration is only human, but don't go making out that you're the new Ronaldo when you're closer to Ali Dia. Football fans, you know exactly what I'm getting at. In fact, the occasional grimace accompanied by some frank self-depreciation never did anybody any harm. It shows people that you're human, but at the same time nobody likes a snivelling wastrel, so keep it humble rather than looking like you're fishing for compliments. Self-depreciation can be most organic through humour, though, so it's worth throwing the occasional jibe out there just to keep people on their toes. However, everyone's humour is completely different, so who am I to say what's funny? There's no joy to be gained from plastic compliments that you force out of people, impress them enough (by being yourself, not by trying too hard to be someone you aren't) and you'll gain the lion's share of compliments as a welcome side-order with your immeasurable comfort in who you are.

There's so much more to discuss when it comes to parties, so many different eventualities that could occur. Luckily, most of these will be covered in subsequent chapters, and anything else that might happen will probably be entirely situational anyway. I think it would be important to stress here that I really don't have all the answers, I'm just a guy trying to help other people feel happy. If something kicks off that you feel completely unprepared for, react. Trust your instincts, stay on your toes, and don't be stupid. If you've got this far then you've got a solid head on your shoulders, keep it that way. Sex and alcohol are two things that we'll move on to, but everybody with reasonable experience in these fields knows that I could write ten books and not say enough about either of these things to prepare anybody for every possible situation. Think on your feet, unless you're swept off them or are too intoxicated to stand up any more.

Chapter 7: DRUGS

'Avoid using cigarettes, alcohol or drugs as alternatives to being an interesting person' – Marilyn Vos Savant

Speaking of intoxication, this is one particular field in which I have absolutely zero experience, and I therefore must offer you, dear reader, a warning that this chapter will contain no empirical evidence of the experience of being drunk or drugged up. I personally have never seen the appeal of either of these pursuits, but that's neither here nor there. It isn't something I'm proud or ashamed of, and while I wouldn't go screaming it from the rooftops, it isn't something that I feel like I need to conceal. As far as I'm concerned, I have just as much fun as everybody else, because in the end it doesn't matter if you're drinking or not. I've heard tales of the warm glow of comfort alcohol in moderation can equip you with, but frankly I feel comfortable enough to not require the support of alcohol to rely on. To those blessed with natural confidence, a clear head makes for an enjoyable evening, plus you get the added bonus of remembering it all the morning after. It's true that a little alcohol can be a boon to those who struggle to open up otherwise, but there's certainly a line between help and hindrance. I've lost count of the number of people who have vented their difficulties to me whilst intoxicated and been enraptured by the coherence of my response, leading to a rapid development of the friendship which I could never have achieved if we'd both been drunk. Having said that, I know plenty a drunkard (one in particular springs to mind) who is completely unlocked by alcohol, his inhibitions lowered and his insightfulness amplified. He's a rare case, however, and he knows enough to keep a lid on how much he's having.

What my own abstinence (I hate to use such a pretentious term, but 'boycott' is no better, and 'avoidance' seems like I have some weird phobia of drinking) has afforded me is an insight into drunk people and their actions. I feel I can safely claim to have experienced more than most the effects that alcohol has on my friends, and I've come to the conclusion that it affects everyone completely differently. I have acquaintances that become much chummier as a result of their drinking, and I have others who get slightly needy and clingy after a little while. While there are a few notable side effects that seem almost universal, I think I'm pretty accurate in saying that everyone's got a different drunk side to them. For some people alcohol can be an ideal social lubricant, allowing for ease of conversation where once there dwelt only awkwardness and anxiety. For others the alcohol consumes them and turns them into a lumbering behemoth of obnoxiousness and destruction. A little of the stuff can help some people out no end; what you've got to be wary of is the 'overdose'.

By this I refer to both drugs and alcohol, actually. I'm not necessarily referring to a single wild night in which you work your liver so hard you should be paying it overtime, but any prolonged period in which you exceed the amount of substances you should be safely putting into your body. I have a friend who has become almost entirely dependent on alcohol to the point that he can't bring himself to go out without drinking anymore, simply because he's become so reliant on it. He completely changes once he's begun to drink, going from shy and retiring to loud and outgoing, the life of most parties. 'Well', I hear you cry, 'what's wrong with that?' Nothing, except for the fact that he requires alcohol to unlock what's already inside him. I can't imagine how much happier this guy would be if he could just be that person all the time, without needing this inebriating key to unlock his personality. As it is, he is a mouse most of the time, who flourishes into a rampaging social elephant on the back of a couple of pints. It's a remarkable transition to witness until you realise that he's lying to himself about his alcohol dependency. Speaking of dependence, I know plenty of people who are convinced that they aren't reliant on cigarettes or marijuana to enjoy themselves. In some ways this is true, they aren't reliant on these things to have fun, at this point they're reliant on them just to feel normal. Some of the brightest students in my school have lost themselves by going off the rails at vital moments, putting drugs and alcohol over their education, and by extension their future. Some people can, admittedly, handle themselves perfectly adequately. They're the lucky ones, because they're able to enjoy the best of both worlds. A great friend of mine is testament to this, able to function on a new level with the aid of drugs, but remaining his amenable self throughout. Unfortunately, people like him are few and far between, much as other people will try to convince you otherwise. Most of us mere mortals have to choose between 'boring' sobriety and the oft-risky state of drunkenness or excessive drug use. I know where I'm putting my standard.

I talked a little bit earlier about the repercussions that inevitably arise once you drink too much, and I feel that this in particular is worth addressing. Be very, VERY careful if you plan to drink your troubles away. One too many and you could end up in a very uncompromising position. I've had the misfortune of witnessing multiple car wrecks along with needless accidents and explicitly unwanted sexual encounters, amongst other things. It isn't worth putting yourself at risk for the sake of forgetting your problems and enjoying the blissful sensation of letting go. Sometimes, it's a lot more admirable to face up to your difficulties and even embrace them. It's hard for me to share this, but probably the main reason why I don't touch any substances is that I feel that in order to live life to the fullest I need to take the bad with the good, the hard times with the easy ones. Drowning your sorrows seems somehow cowardly, and I feel as though dealing with my problems personally rather than relying on Jack Daniels to do it for me has turned me into a much more level-headed person. I must reiterate here that because this works for me is no reason to expect that it'll work for anybody else. Everybody will have a different solution to this particular problem, and it just so happens that sobriety is mine.

As a welcome side effect of this, a lot of people entrust me with keeping an eye on them once they start drinking. This may sound like a drag, but it's a nice feeling knowing your friends trust you enough to know that you have their very best interests at heart. In the event that anything does happen, I'm alert enough to deal with the situation. I'd offer a single piece of advice to anyone considering my approach: stick to your guns. People will inevitably offer you drinks, and some may even be uncompromising in their pursuit of your drunkenness. I feel like for a lot of people the fact that somebody isn't drinking makes them somehow uncomfortable, like you're judging them by remaining sober, or at a temporary intellectual advantage. Perhaps they believe you have more control than they do, something which I'm sure is completely disconcerting. As a final word on this subject, I think it is important to ensure that people do what is right for them. This chapter was never intended to be an anti-drug pamphlet, and I hope that readers can take this information on board and make their own decision about the best course of action in these kinds of situations. All I can say is that I have a much better time having a laugh at my own lack of ability on the dance floor, chatting to complete strangers about their past and pushing the limits of accepted social chatter, all entirely sober, than my friends do vomiting into their hair before kissing multiple strangers and collapsing in a pool of confusion and self-loathing after one too many.

Chapter 8: SEX

'Sex without love is merely healthy exercise'

– Robert A. Heinlein

Given the abundance of teenage promiscuity these days, it seems more likely than not that most people will engage in a little 'how's-your-father' before they're 20. This is almost universally regarded as a good thing, and I'm not about to disagree with that. After all, there's a lot to be said for the therapeutic qualities a good night of sexual conquest with a partner of your choice. However, it must be noted that the seemingly old-fashioned mantra of 'waiting for someone you love' really is the best way to go about things. There's a lot to be said for getting your first time out of the way, notably that you'll be 'better', or at least more experienced, by the time you find someone you really love. Frankly, if they love you back they aren't going to care how good or bad you were. If all that they cared about was a quick burst of endorphins, they would've stayed at home with a copy of Playboy and a jar of Vaseline for company.

An important thing to remember about this particular activity is that it really doesn't matter as much as everyone says. When you're young, every other conversation ends up in a discussion of 'who's been the furthest', or 'who's had the most girl/boyfriends'. This reaches a pinnacle once you hit fifteen or sixteen, with people falling over themselves for the 'pride' of being able to say they went to 'third base' with the attractive stranger they met half an hour ago. From a sober point of view, it's clear to see that this is neither classy nor laudable. Nevertheless, I've known people who don't realise this fact for years and years, having sex with the first guy or girl to show them a little attention all the while. I still know people who fit this mould, and would rather have sex with a different person every night of the week than someone they really like. I struggle to understand this point of view, as past the age of about 23 nobody with more than a handful of brain cells is going to care about how many partners you've had.

When it comes down to a serious relationship, everyone is different. Some of the best partnerships can blossom out of a one-night stand, and my own personal experience has told me that it's impossible to judge someone on the actions of any one night. Some couples I know have sex every day, for others twice a month is a push. It's about finding out what works for you, and adapting accordingly. My advice with regards to being happy is not to worry about it. I consider sex as an expression of your feelings for someone rather than an explosive release of pent up aggression, and I feel that's how it should be. If that really is all you're looking for then I know plenty of girls that'd be up for that, just don't expect any emotional connection afterwards. 'Great!' resonates the chorus of male readers. But I urge all those thinking this is a sweet deal to reconsider: in actuality these conquests, while enjoyable, are short-lived and highly emotionally charged. Don't come running to me once you've been dropped for the next piece of meat your former concubine wants to get on now that it's a new day/week/month. What really makes you feel good is the bond you can establish with someone once you get really close to them. You'll find that other potential squeezes get a lot less desirable once you've got the best sponge in the whole damn bucket.

Another point about sex that really resonates with me is that it should be something private. Keep what happens between you and your significant other on the down low, not least because there are very few people who will take kindly to being regaled with endless stories of your afternoon antics if they aren't getting any themselves. Talking explicitly about sex always seems to undermine the serene quality it has, and a fateful encounter that is reduced to a conversation piece over dinner gains an undesirable quality of lewdness and loses everything that made it special in the first place. It's so tempting to boast endlessly about your exploits, especially when they're either impressive or unprecedented, but once you've found someone you truly care about, you'll value the incomparable intimacy a lot more than any small semblance of admiration gleamed from some small-minded underlings so desperate for closeness that even hearing about somebody else's sex life makes them feel a little better. Leave these folks to their vicarious masturbation.

One key thing to mention on the subject of sex is the chasm of difference between sex and sex as portrayed by the industry. Porn, to be frank, is not an adequate representation of what real sex is like. Without going into graphic detail, there is barely anything on the internet that will directly correlate with the sex any of us is likely to have, from the way girls/guys look to the way they act. To be perfectly honest I am glad of this fact. As exciting as internet sex seems to be, there's no romance there, and it's all too obvious that the second the camera goes off whatever spark may have been there fizzles out remarkably fast. Personally, I'd be more inclined to favour the type of sex where the nails dig into your back purely out of lust, rather than because the nasally Texan director said so.

Veering to the complete opposite end of the scale to those who view sex as a necessary, animalistic release that merely has the added bonus of feeling pretty good at the same time, we find those who devote themselves wholeheartedly to anybody they sleep with. They'll replay the moment in their minds a thousand times, immortalise the experience in a dozen Shakespearian sonnets and never sleep again, just so that the day can last forever. Frankly, this is unhealthy. If sex with someone really is this Earth-shattering, my advice is to slap a wedding ring on their finger and get them down the aisle before they quite comprehend what's going on. It's all too easy to fall into this trap, especially near the beginning of one's sexual 'career'. A sad fact of life is that the vast majority of first relationships aren't going to go the distance no matter how hard you try. Sealing the deal with sex purely to utilise this event as a justification to yourself to stay with someone that isn't right for you is definitely sex for the wrong reasons. Be honest with yourself in your actions: Don't have sex with really drunk people because you're really drunk and because it seems to be 'the done thing'. Don't let your opinion be swayed by fairy tales and put all of yourself into one person just to figure out they're not right for you, and stubbornly stay with them anyway, whispering reassuring falsehoods to yourself all the while. Have sex with the people you really love, because you really love them, to show them just how much you love them. And enjoy it.

Chapter 9: WORK

'A dream doesn't become a reality through magic. It takes sweat, determination, and hard work'

– Colin Powell

In my experience, one of the hardest things to bring myself to do is work. Be it schoolwork, paid work or (God forbid) housework, it's never fun to subject yourself to the tedium of these repetitive tasks when you could be doing something much more fun and productive. Time after time I find myself sitting idly at my desk, reading the same paragraph over and over again because it simply will not go in. I'm sure readers will sympathise rather than judge when I say that deep down I am a lazy sod who would rather sit on his arse all day than do something as mind-bendingly tedious as actual work. At my school we're recommended six hours of work per day in the few months leading up to exams. Frankly, I can't think of anything worse. It's tough enough sitting through three or four lessons a day (how my younger self ever managed six I will never know) in a scholastic environment but asking me to sit at home in a nest of paper, surrounded by what feels like half a library's worth of books is paramount to asking a goldfish to quickly nip down the road and pick some groceries. He wouldn't remember the list, never mind come back with the goods.

I've found (through hours of rigmarole and more than a handful of tried and tested techniques) that there is no one way to sit down and get something done. Sorry to burst that particular bubble, but to me it seems as though this is another case in which everyone is different. It helps to have a goal, something to focus on as a sort of light at the end of a particularly arduous tunnel. Often even this isn't enough, and I find myself staring blankly at words on a page until they stop looking like words anymore. Obviously, depending on the goal, you may be more or less motivated to do something. If there's a University-place shaped fruit on the tree you're climbing, that's obviously going to feel like the particular job you're undertaking is worth your while. If all you're going to get out of the job is a couple of quid from your neighbour for mowing his lawn, you may be tempted to just leave the bit round the corner that he can't immediately see. However, deep down we all know that you'd be better off doing an immaculate job for the whole place, no matter how much effort you'll have to muster.

Without being hypocritical, one thing that can aid your work hugely with regards to work is being in the correct state of mind. Some people may work better in certain environments but without the Zen-like state of focus nobody is going to do anything worthwhile. For some, this is associated with a certain area in which they work, and only work. That much is vital: to designate an area for working in, and to not allow any distractions to penetrate the force field of learning you construct around it. When it comes to work, videogames and text messages are not your friend. Be sure to tell those friends who just won't let up with the contact that you're working, and stick to your guns about it. It's all too easy to get caught up in a message-fest with someone you barely have the time of day for usually but is nevertheless much more interesting than that Maths paper you've been putting off all day. I know it sounds like I'm regaling you with the same advice your teachers give you on a daily basis, but the only way you're going to get anywhere is personalised self-discipline. An example might be a reward system, or playing music to encourage focus. Everybody will learn in a different way.

To start with, some people might need their own work zone to be in a specific place, say near a window. Personally, being so terrible at work is probably not helped by the fact that I use my desk for everything, be it writing or schoolwork. I can't help but feel that setting aside an area would've raised my productivity no end. Music is marmite here: it'll either help you focus your thoughts entirely and get really productive, or distract you to the point where you drop the pencil and lose yourself in the song. In subjects where a high level of concentration at all times is required, I wouldn't recommend it, but for more creative work I've found it successful, and some of my best essays have been written with the aid of slow, melodious songs without lyrics. This should also be your only companion if you seriously plan on getting something done. I find it impossible to work even with someone else in the room, never mind trying to teach each other things. Solitary and sorrowful it may be, but sitting by yourself behind a work desk can yield real results where casually 'working' at a friend's house has failed so many times before.

When it comes down to it, pushing past the ten-minute mark really propels you forward when working. It usually takes about that long to settle down into the work you're doing and avoid the all-too tempting drag of distractions. Some people work best in the evening around dusk, others function much better in the ungodly hours of the morning. My advice here would be to err on the side of caution and only work in a framework of around 16 hours, say 7am to around 11pm. Beyond that, you're unlikely to be focused enough to get anything done, and before you'll be too blurry-eyed to even see what you're supposed to be working on. Never ever pull all-nighters when you start to panic about your lack of work, you may as well be asleep for the amount of productive work you'll complete. It's painful, it's boring, and it's a bitch to do for any extended length of time, but working will eventually return all the favours you do it. Most of the time you get out of it what you put in, so don't expect a wedding cake of results if all you put in was some rotten eggs and the milk the goldfish forgot to bring back.

On a personal level, I've never felt the same sense of accomplishment as when I've seen the fruits of my work culminate into something great. I once had a short play I'd written performed, and to see the work come to life really is something else. Academic achievements, too, culminate in a similar sense of swelling pride that leaves you safe in the knowledge that hard work yields results. Working your arse off to get into a top University means that feeling when you open the envelope and finally get the offer hits you all the harder. It's an incomparable rush, and the only way you'll get there is by putting in the hours. If that's not what you're aiming for, the rush translates across accomplishments and bridges boundaries. It takes character to stick at the same task for hours on end, but I'm sure anybody reading this book has that in spades. Now put it to good use.

Chapter 10: HOBBIES

'My hobbies just sort of gradually became my vocation'

– 'Weird' Al Yankovic

Veering wildly to the other end of the spectrum, it is of no less importance to ensure that spare time is spent as carefully and meticulously as work time. Anybody without a designated hobby, something to do in their spare time, faces the imminent threat of boredom every single hour that they aren't working. If you fear that you may be one of these people, take up something. Make it a worthwhile excursion, preferably something you can be really proud of. However, be sure to make it a pastime that you enjoy. There's no point blowing all your free time on an impressive hobby if you leave yourself no time for having fun, the key is balance. Maintain a reasonable work ethic but leave yourself enough time on the weekends to go deep-sea angling, kite surfing or dragon boat racing, whatever's your poison. Don't get caught up in the concept of a desperate requirement to work hard, neglecting all opportunities for fun as you go. Let's be honest, being a workaholic is neither fun nor entirely healthy: be reasonable with yourself and let go every once in a while.

I work as hard as I can during the week to ensure I have the weekends off to do as I please. This system works because it leaves you with something to look forward to when the week's work is racking up, and gives you the impetus to complete it all to maintain the sanctity of those glorious two days of liberty. I find a change of scenery on the weekends can do wonders for my mood, and I always come back to school feeling refreshed and ready to undertake another week of hard graft and toil. It helps to just see friends that you don't see every day; remember all those friends you made at parties back in Chapter Six? See them, keep them close to you; they're invaluable as a means of relaxation on days where you want to complete distance yourself from the humdrum tedium of scholastic life. I probably see my outside friends three times as much as I see my school friends on weekends. Balance, this time between different types of friends, is again the byword here. If you only ever see the same people day after day they're eventually going to become dull and uninteresting to you, harsh as that sounds. Branch out, before the twig you're currently on snaps under your weight.

Personally, I find solace in reading and writing. I can't get enough of either of these excursions (do you really think I'd be writing a book instead of doing something normal if I didn't *really* enjoy it?). I try to do as much of each of them as I can. School aside, I'm a huge football fan, which serves as a welcome distraction on days where the written word can't quite fill the hole in my heart that yearns for a distraction. I find having a smorgasbord of different hobbies helps keep life entertaining and invigorating and, whilst watching football for hours every weekend may not be entirely constructive, that's what my writing and reading is for. Keeping the scales even between hobbies that are purely practised for the sake of having a good time and those that actively create something (or act as a means to an end, like learning to be a Grade 8 musician or a world-class gymnast) allows you to have a good time, relax enough to focus on work when needs be and, above all, be happy.

If you follow through on something you enjoy, you could be lucky enough to make a career out of it. Whilst the number of musical geniuses that eventually go on to make it in the big leagues is low, there nevertheless remains a niche in the market for those brave enough to take a risk on something they love. Frankly, I can't imagine a better career than one in which I do something that I love day after day. I can't see myself getting bored of a job that gives me this much freedom to do as I please. That kind of motivation to turn something you enjoy into something you get paid to do means that it's relatively easy to urge yourself into pursuing a hobby to the highest level. Sure, some days it will feel like the last thing you want to do is get home from school just to practise your piano for a few hours, but once you're on stage in front of thousands of people ready to listen to your work, it all seems worth it. This may sound unrealistic but it really does happen, and thousands of people have found the loophole in life that allows them to do an enjoyable job that earns them enough money to live on.

Finding a hobby that requires other people is even better. An out of school club allows you the opportunity to make even more friends, with similar interests to you. It's really liberating to find others who think the same way that you do. It doesn't matter in cases like these if your hobby is something ludicrously obscure, because there's inevitably going to be other people who share your interest. Never again will you be crippled by the choice between friends and your hobby, because there are hundreds of people out there who feel just as excited by the pursuit as you do. If your hobby, like mine, is more of a solitary activity, that's fine too. It doesn't matter if the activity itself is something you do by yourself, there's still no limit to the amount that you can share with other people, if you're so inclined. There are dozens of websites devoted to each and every pastime going, so you don't even have to leave the house. There's no excuse to not be a part of a wholesome and welcoming community that centres on something you really enjoy. Share your interest (and talent!) with other people and you'll be surprised at the dividends: support, criticism and friends await those who go looking for them.

The value of pursuing that which you're interested in really cannot be stated enough. If nothing else, it acts as a distraction from the more tedious aspects of life and at best it's something you spend all day looking forward to doing. Make sure your hobbies stay interesting and don't become a chore, and you'll be well set to enjoy life a whole lot more. Having something to focus on that isn't work and actually makes you feel good is invaluable. Be proud of what you do, stick it to the man and keep practicing your origami if it's really your passion: don't let anybody tell you that paper craft isn't the greatest hobby ever when to you it absolutely is.

Chapter 11: AMBITION

'Intelligence without ambition is a bird without wings'

– Salvador Dali

Of course, to expect all sorts of wonderful things to simply fall into your lap is both short-sighted and irrational. There are three facets you simply must indulge in order to achieve what you desire: commitment, ambition, and perseverance. Without these traits to accompany you it's all too easy to fall off the metaphorical wagon and leave things unfinished more often than not. Personally, I've always struggled with commitment and my notebook is saturated with half-complete poems and short stories I never got around to finishing and probably never will. It seems to me that the reason behind this is a combination of two factors. The first is that the majority of these stories were conceived out of boredom rather than motivation, and the second that most of them weren't much good to start with anyway. Everything worth achieving necessitates hard graft, unless you're one of the blessed few who are able to conjure consistently impressive work seemingly out of thin air, like some jammy folks I've had the misfortune of knowing. For most of us, however, a little elbow grease is required to get the ball rolling.

In every walk of life playing the nonchalant card will get you a decent pay-out but committing to a cause and sticking to it is what really earns you the big bucks. Take friendships. In most cases you get out exactly what you put in; meaning that in those instances wherein you simply coast along and greedily consume all that someone else has to offer whilst sacrificing nothing of your own, no bonafide friendship can be born. If, on the other hand, you're willing to put yourself on the line for people, compromise and trust somebody, you'll make yourself a fine friend indeed and be stood in good stead for making more. I can't think of any true friend of mine that hasn't sacrificed a lot to be in that position. This may sound like some sort of initiation ritual and I suppose in a sense it is and should be. I believe that a real friendship is forged in a hot kiln of exertion and sweat. A few days of chatter does not a friendship make; real friends go through Hell and high water to develop a lasting bond that won't snap at the first sign of discomfort. On that point, I also don't have any friends that I haven't argued with on occasion. It's important to challenge the friends you do have if they do or say something that you disagree with;

otherwise resentment builds. Flag people up if they offend you or someone close to you, but make absolutely sure to rebuild the connection as soon as the issue has been resolved. Seething in a corner for months on end waiting for an apology just leads to grief for all involved. Be true to your friends and persevere with the people you're close to when times get tough. If these connections broke down every time an argument took place, the world would be a much more irritating and much less enjoyable place to live in.

Little things can give you the most motivation. I wrote a quotation that I've never told anyone about on a little piece of paper that I look at every time I need that extra boost to complete something important. These sorts of things are very personal and I couldn't start to tell anybody how to build up their own motivational stash, but a word of advice is to pick things that stick with you the first time you hear them and continue to make you think on the third or fourth time. Something with that much sticking power often constitutes a maxim you'd be willing to apply to your own life. Again, creating a list of goals can help you envisage the place in which you could realistically be if you pulled your finger out and really strived to get where you need to be. Ignore the trivial things and commit to those pursuits that matter: high scores on whatever videogame happens to be current and popular won't do you much good later in life. Hell, they aren't even going to be relevant when the sequel comes out! I think here I must mention the motivation of others and the act of persuading those unable to motivate themselves. Your friends might not thank you for lecturing them on the benefits of hard work but once they realise that being bone-idle all day every day won't get them anywhere, they'll appreciate your stern words.

When it comes to the future, never place a limit on what you can achieve. It's imperative to do what you want with your life, as long as that doesn't involve the annihilation of anybody else's plans, of course. If you genuinely and realistically believe you have the commitment and passion to become a best-selling author, a world-renowned speaker or a ruthless politician, don't let anybody poo-poo your desires. You know full well that accomplishments like this need hard graft and a whole lot of luck, but if you manage the controllable factors, take risks when you have to and put yourself out there, then there really isn't any reason why anybody can't be the next great success story of our time. Even if your aims are slightly less grand and all you want is a well-paying job and a happy family, a bit of ambition helps all the more in achieving these things.

Be unceasingly stubborn when it comes to your dreams. People will always tell you that there are some things that normal folk weren't ever meant to do, but I can't get on board with that attitude. If people really never pushed themselves then nothing important would ever get done. Imagine the world we'd be living in if people all consigned themselves to a life of bland toil and never took a chance on something they really wanted to try, but may have had a certain degree of risk associated with it. Imagine if Stephen Hawking had just given up because of his condition: the world would have lost one of the greatest minds of the modern era. Imagine a world where Einstein kept his 'steady' job as a clerk in a patent office. A world where Abraham Lincoln died as just another poor boy. What I'm trying to say is anybody can make anything of themselves if they're willing to pry their fingers off the remote, heartily crack their knuckles and set to work trying to squeeze every drop of life from existence. We only get a few short years here, and I plan to make the most of mine.

Chapter 12: READING

'Reading is to the mind what exercise is to the body'

- Steele

If you'll indulge me, reader, I'd like to take some time out of ranting to tell a story about reading, and the importance of it. I can't stress enough how much I think everybody should read, no matter what it is. The first book I ever read that really resonated with me with Oscar Wilde's 'The Picture of Dorian Gray'. Before that I had always stuck to books that were easy to finish without much input from the reader. I found myself unable to put down the Wilde, determined to follow the author's reasonably complex prose. I even found myself laughing out loud at some points, I was that immersed in the story. When you read a book that really makes you feel something, you'll never forget it. I have a real passion for reading that I've only really pursued in the last few years, and there's a special kind of spellbinding emotion that accompanies witnessing a true work of art spill its contents into your psyche.

When I was younger, I never stopped reading. Granted, my library contained more 'Where's Wally?' than 'Wuthering Heights', but I was reading nonetheless. I'm still convinced my terrible vision is a result of too many late nights under the covers, eyes straining to see the words (or Wally) in the darkness. Eventually, a combination of an ever-decreasing supply of free-time, a desire to spend said free time otherwise employed and a couple of other things led to my reading faculty lying dormant for several years. I was more focused on the standard teenage pursuits: girls and popularity. Looking back, I really regret the years of potentially undisturbed reading that I missed out upon. That's a lot of wasted hours that I would rather have given to Austen or Hardy than the issues I ended up worrying about instead.

I am forever indebted to my family for reintroducing me to this pursuit. A little while back, I became really committed to chasing a spot at a high-ranking University, and decided a copious helping of reading outside my course could only better my chances. Philosophy, my degree of choice, has arguably the largest body of writing surrounding it bar English, so it wasn't as though I would struggle to find something suitable. Of course, as with any subject, you can't drop yourself immediately in at the deep end; you have to learn to walk before you can run. I started with a few introductory texts in Philosophy and moved on quickly to harder stuff. It's amazing how little time it takes to fall back into a habit again. Over the course of a few months I had devoured more texts and decided to ask my grandmother for a certain book I had been looking for and couldn't find. Sure enough, I received a parcel in the post a few days later. Contained within the package was the book I had requested — Cervantes' 'Don Quixote' — with yellowed pages and a fragile spine. The note attached read thusly: 'Harry, here is your grandfather's book. Love Granny'.

In order to explain the significance of this message I have to venture a little way back into my family history. My biological grandfather died a long time before I was born, meaning (of course) that I never knew him. I'm told that I'm a lot like him, which is a nice thing to hear. He was liked by all until his premature death, and was someone with a lot of status in the community. An Oxford Don, it's a strange coincidence that I happened to unknowingly apply to the same college he had represented in life. Taken from his family far too early, he died at the age of 26. Much as I love my remaining grandparents, I have always regretted the fact that I never knew this one. Just knowing this book had belonged to him meant it came with a lot of symbolic value, and opening the front cover to see his signature staring back at me gave me shivers, along with the date: May, 1956. More than 50 years have passed since then, and still I feel his presence within the pages. I'll never treasure as book as much as this one, and it hasn't left my bedside since the day I received it.

If this chapter seems more autobiographical than others, it's because I feel this might be the only way to reach out to people when it comes to something like reading. I can't force anybody to read something, and doing so is not on the same level as getting somebody to watch a film you think they'd enjoy. People are much more willing to give up two hours rather than two weeks of their time. Reading means so much to me because I see it as a link to the past, allowing a dramatic insight into the mind of the author in a way that no TV show or film ever could. Reading a book means allowing your imagination to conjure up images and construct scenarios instead of having them presented to you on a silver platter (or screen). There's nothing that can compare to a great book for me; they really are works of art every bit as much as paintings or architecture. When I die, my biggest regret will surely be not reading enough books. 'Dorian Gray' meant so much to me because it gave me that sense of accomplishment when I turned the last page, and looking back over the path I'd ventured down, hand in hand with a long-dead author's thoughts, I was filled an emotion unlike any other.

I always reserve a couple of hours every night before I go to bed for reading. Immersing yourself completely in a book is an unparalleled joy, and comes with innumerable benefits. I forget everything I may have worried about that day, and deadlines and exams fade to nothingness. It's a gateway to another world right at your fingertips, and every new book is merely another chapter in your own personal odyssey into the wild world of literature. From Cervantes to Shakespeare, Plato to Peacock, Melville to Dr. Seuss, the ocean of literature embodies the knowledge and creativity of generations, and will continue to delight and enthral generations to come. I can't think of anything better to aspire to than to one day be spoken of in the same breath as some of these, the finest minds the world has ever seen.

Chapter 13: WORDS

'Words are the only things that last forever'

-William Hazlitt

The title of this chapter may be something of a misnomer. This chapter will not be dedicated purely to the art of eloquence, but I felt such a word accurately encapsulated what I am attempting to convey in this chapter, that is, the importance of stretching the English language as far as it will go, and then stretching it some more. In my view, the vocabulary of most modern people is vastly underwhelming, a fact I feel needs immediate correction as soon as possible. If English teachers would utilise a fraction of their time to expanding the lexis of their classes, the English-speaking world would be all the more stimulating and exciting.

The first step towards achieving this ideal, I feel, is to confront my readers directly and admit to a certain obsession of mine, namely the English language. Despite its inherent stupidity at times and almost unassailable grammatical idioms, it has served me well in my years of using it and I feel it would be impossibly hard to express my thoughts without it. To quote a great playwright, and one of my personal favourites, 'words are all we have'. Beckett is making a bold statement here, and though it might be a common thought that words are nothing more than labels for our otherwise incommunicable thoughts, a jumble of noises assigned to a particular thought or object, this viewpoint is one I vehemently reject. I feel that the definitions that we *have* agreed upon (the life's work of some linguistics-obsessed goblins in the labyrinth of Oxford's libraries) should not be so quickly eschewed, and should instead be appreciated, lauded even.

I don't think enough people take advantage of the many weird and wonderful words we've been gifted by history. I believe that a lot of reading really helps to widen one's sphere in cases such as these, as authors tend to get bored with the run-of-the-mill words and throw in a couple of grandiloquent phrases (I'm sorry, I promise I'll stop) every now and then, which readers subsequently pick up on and feel they have to research and understand. It's a quintessentially human quality. I must admit, however, that I've definitely been one to abuse language and use words that are quite frankly inappropriate in an effort to make myself sound more knowledgeable. Whilst this chapter might make me sound like a fool with an overinflated ego and the ability to go on thesaurus.com, it's written with tongue firmly in cheek. The key to sounding like you know what you're talking about is control and comprehension, not complexity.

Being well spoken gets you places. That's the long and short of it and it seems to me there is no benefit to be gleamed from not having an extensive hoard of words to call upon at every opportunity. People the world over are impressed with someone who can speak confidently and select his words carefully, be it in writing or in person. I have no doubts that a significant portion of my (admittedly meagre) success is due to the hours I've put in researching unconventional words and trying to incorporate them into my vocabulary. The beautiful thing about this language is that nobody has a complete knowledge of it, and even someone with the most effective memory in the world could never be aware of every definition and meaning. One reason for this is that language is in itself so protean; consistently shifting with the ages so that just as a word comes into colloquial usage another slips out. Language creeps slowly rather than barrelling into us, and it's interesting to look at the etymology of words we use every day.

To reinforce my earlier point, being eloquent doesn't always mean utilising the longest or most impressive words possible, but rather the words that work with the situation at hand. Sometimes a lot more can be said with simple, powerful words rather than tongue-twisters that sounds nice in the right hands (or mouths). Monosyllabic words often carry much more weight than lengthier ones, so if I say 'To be or not to be' (whilst simultaneously completely undermining my earlier argument about the fact that Shakespeare is overused) it resonates with a lot more poignancy than 'To exist or not to exist', or even 'To prevail or not to prevail'. I'll stop now. My point is that the right word is not always the most complicated, and despite the saturation of this chapter with complex phraseology, I sincerely believe that (for the most part).

On the topic of phraseology (a word I consistently fail to spell correctly, those double vowels will be the death of me) we arrive at the impasse of spelling. From what I've seen some people just can't spell, and that's okay. Sure, it grinds my gears to see the infamous 'your/you're' perplexity, but in the end it has to be water off a duck's back. Language is something fun, fascinating and ripe for new and exciting utilisation. Just don't abuse it, or risk sounding like just another pedantic chat-show host with a degree in douchebaggery (okay, that one I made up).

Chapter 14: PARENTS

'Lovers grow cold, men learn to hate their wives, and only parents' love can last out lives'

– Browning

When you're young, your parents know everything. How to fix what you're convinced is a broken knee (but turns out to be a minor graze,) how to pronounce that ludicrously long word (good old 'impossible' living up to its name in reading terms,) and even, as the years went by, how to fix a broken heart (read: damaged pride.) As a youngster your parents are as close to real-life superheroes as you're ever going to find. They're the ones who instil the values you'll subconsciously maintain for the rest of your life, and to some it may seem that they spend half their lives telling you what to do and, perhaps more often, what not to do. In my view, the value of parents differs between individual families as each set has something brand new to offer their sprogs: a new brand of parenting. Only having one set of (bonafide) parents means I can only offer my own experiences, and I must stress that not all parents are the same. I count myself incredibly lucky to have had the upbringing I did, as I feel a lot of what I personally value is down to their influence.

In my view, parents should be seen as allies rather than enemies. So many people seem to harbour deep-seated resentment for their parents, which I'll admit is in some cases justified. I'm very lucky to have the parents that I do, and whilst I've sometimes seen them as the pure embodiment of evil I know that they have my best interests at heart. They're great people and until recently I naively thought that everybody had been blessed with such a fabulous hand in life. Unfortunately that isn't true and plenty of people struggle with their parents on a daily basis, over things that are never their fault. I can't imagine what it's like to be one of these children, and I can only say that I'm immensely fortunate not to be one. Some of the most well-rounded people I know had terrible upbringings and it's only forced them into being better people (and often better parents) themselves. It seems as though there sometimes is a silver lining to an unfair childhood.

Let's face it, having children is stressful and raising them exponentially more so. I tip my hat to any parents, and especially appreciate my own, for going through such a harrowing process, and I'm quite frankly shocked that mine aren't much worse off following the experience. Every parent that devotes themselves to raising a child deserves a huge amount of credit for their commitment, something that seems to go missing in too many cases nowadays. Good parents are there to make you flourish, allow you to spread your wings and achieve your dream. One of the worst things a parent can do is to try and force their child into doing something that they themselves are interested in, rather than what the child wants to do. Apathy or even excessive negativity are qualities that are even worse in parents, and those who don't even try to help their kids flourish don't deserve acclaim in the slightest. It's hard for me to see things from that point of view, but I've met more than a few people who have fought tooth and nail to turn themselves into incredible characters despite their parents' best efforts to quash them. I suppose, when it comes down to it, it's a lottery. Some people luck out with the best possible parents and others get apathetic, neglectful or downright torturous ones. Having said that, I feel strongly that discipline is important and focus entirely necessary. Parents who let their kids get away with murder are bad, and worse are those who put their foot down excessively. It's so important to respect your parents when they do their job right. They're older and, in most cases, wiser than you, so there really aren't any grounds for the all-too-frequent occurrences of 'kid power' wherein a parent will buckle under pressure from a tyrannical teenager and act submissive for a while, bending to his/her every whim. Anything for a quiet life. Of course, parents step out of line too, and I know plenty of tyrannical Mums and Dads who are far worse than their children. Those who try their best, however, really put their heart and soul into making you a better person.

For me, this encapsulates the best way to think about parents. Consider them as wealthy benefactors and of yourself as an author. They've invested a whole lot of time and energy into you, and so you had better come out with something to show for it or risk huge disappointment, not from your parents, who will be proud of every achievement no matter how slight, but from yourself. The most inspiring viewpoint on parents is to see them as the springboard to your success. Never forget where you come from, and be proud of the people who made you who you are. Sometimes it seems to take people a few years to really understand just how much their parents do for them, and how much gratitude that really warrants.

When it comes down to it, your parents are your rock. It's another cliché to say so, but your friends come and go whilst family is always there. Growing up I've learnt to recognise shortcomings in my parents and actually have ended up liking them more as people as a result. I'm very dissimilar in a lot of ways to both my father and my mother, but I still manage to get on well with them, and the things we do share are committed to wholeheartedly by both parties. Once you start treating your parents like people rather than machines I strongly believe things become much more relaxed, parents settle into an advisory guardian role and are happy to view their children's progress as they become what they were always capable of being.

If my parents weren't my parents I feel like I would be friends with them anyway. I think that says everything about my relationship with them. The issue is, not everybody has parents like mine, and I realise that. Almost all of my closest friends have struggled with their parents at points, and been completely in the right whilst doing it. This chapter might seem absolutely one-sided, but you only get one set of parents. Mine are fun-loving and the perfect platform for me and my sister to move on to bigger and better things. The important thing is becoming your own person and if you have their support then fantastic. If you don't, you'll just have to be all the stronger in rallying against suppression and truly turning your life around.

Chapter 15: MONEY

'Money, which is of very uncertain value, and sometimes has no value at all, and even less'

– Carlyle

In the past, avarice has led to nothing less than the downfall of empires. King James was notorious for his extravagance, which caused near-irreparable damage to the English economy in the early seventeenth century. Murder, suicide and worse have sprung out of monetary disputes. I suppose it really is true what they say about moolah: want of money is the root of all evil. Well, in a sense. Money is what you make of it, there's nothing inherently cruel about paper and coins. Just like beauty, I think the value (or lack thereof) of money is what you decide it to be. The problem lies in figuring out just how important it actually is. I've struggled to keep a balance in the past between saving and spending, and I always felt worried whenever I splashed out on something I didn't expressly need. I spoke in the last chapter about the value of parental advice and one of the greatest tips my Dad ever gave me was never to worry about money, at least not more than absolutely necessary. Some people have it and some don't. Some have more than others, some save when others spend, and a lot of people worry far too much about something they can't change.

While I believe it's true that being born in to a wealthy family can, on occasions dependant on a huge number of other factors including parents, ambition, talent and so on, constitute naturally the best start in life available, it's important to recognise that you can't change the start you have any more than you can change your race. If you weren't one of the fortunate few to be gifted a head start in life, deal with it. There's no point aspiring to become something that you aren't. On the other hand, self-made millionaires are rife on the scene these days, and rags-to-riches stories maintain as much popularity as they ever had. The key difference that I have noticed between these two groups is that one side, (with some notable exceptions) those who inherit their wealth, typically take it for granted and consider themselves to have some sort of entitlement to better treatment as a result. Those who earn their fortune strike me as much more humble and likeable, and seem to value what they have a lot more. Of course, this sweeping statement won't apply to everyone, and I'm sure there are plenty of self-made millionaires that I'd rather not spend my time with if I can help it. On the other hand, I know a couple of people who came from money who I absolutely adore, and couldn't pick out as being rich at all if I didn't know that about them. It's something that's completely dependent on other factors, I'm just saying that the stereotype can be (and is often) fulfilled in these cases.

It's important to recognise that money really can't bring you happiness. People convince themselves that by surrounding themselves with things they'll feel better as a person, but when it comes down to it there's no substitute for the things that really make you happy: Love, comfort, an enjoyable life in which you flourish and enjoy your career. These are the things that really matter. Having a job you love that pays reasonably is infinitely better than working long hours at a job you hate just to have a little spending money. When it comes down to it you aren't going to be on your deathbed thinking about all the money you might have made, you'll be thinking how you wasted the vast majority of your able life sitting behind a desk while the world passed you by. Clichés aside, don't work all your years and wait for life to fall into your lap, (oops, that's another) go out and grab it by the balls.

I believe that it's vital to strike the right balance between spending and saving. Keep enough in your bank account to ensure that you'll be comfortable in the event of a disaster, but not so much that you frequently have to stop yourself from buying small things that take your fancy. Another gem from my parents is to always save ten per cent of your salary no matter what happens. If you can keep this up, you'll always have a little cushion of security to fall back on, and it means you'll still have a significant chunk of your salary to sink your teeth into even after everyday necessities are taken care of. Setting aside a certain percentage means you never have to spend hours toiling over bills and having to carefully structure fun activities always lessens the amount of enjoyment you gleam from them.

The thing about money is that it's a means to an end, a truth that often eludes people. You don't value money for what it actually is because at the end of the day it's just a few pieces of paper or metal with fancy drawings on them. What people really value is what money brings them, a comfortable and happy life. People should be grateful for what money allows them, yes, but this shouldn't elevate the cash itself onto a pedestal. It's demoralising to hear some people wax lyrical about the repercussions that emerge once the money well dries up: stories of broken marriages and depression strike me as short-sighted when it comes to the grander things in life. I don't think I'd personally marry anybody who I suspected would leave me if my wages dried up, because salary is not and never will be a healthy criterion on which to base attraction in my book. Money itself can, of course, open doors for other problems, but its value is not dependant on the numbers in the account, but rather the trying effect that not having it has on everything else. Money should be a tool that we begrudgingly accept as simply part of life. People have told me they would rather be rich and unhappy than broke and happy, but to me that just sounds so wrong. In my view, happiness always has to come before anything else. Relentlessly pursuing money can lead to both physical and mental detriment and I'd much rather passively respect with reasonable awe the impact and power of money whilst never paying too much heed to it than be constantly chasing more of it.

Greed is one of the most unattractive qualities in people. Seeing someone's eyes metaphorically turn to dollar signs at the sight of a thick wad of cash is, frankly, embarrassing. If the most exciting thing in your life is the Queen's face on a crinkly piece of paper with a hologram then you need some serious reassessment. I keep just enough money in my wallet as I know I'll need, which means I never need to worry about overspending or being caught short. Plus, added bonus, my wallet's lighter. As a teenager, I'm very aware that my money troubles probably haven't even started yet, and this chapter is almost exclusively aimed at people like me in that sense. It's a sad fact of life that people have genuine monetary wants and issues, and these are problems that I can't begin to wrap my head around yet. I guess the message I'm trying to put out here is that you shouldn't try and grow up too fast when it comes to money, because the issues will continue to worsen the older you get. Take a walk, be outside, and leave the worrying to your adult self.

Chapter 16: MUSIC

'Rugged the breast that music cannot tame'

— J. C. Bampflyde

Music is probably the biggest industry in the world, and for good reason. Over the millennia since some troglodyte whittled a piece of wood and blew through it to make noises, music has had an almost unparalleled influence on society. From Mozart's enduring legacy to the rap movements of 90s USA, entire epochs have come to be characterised by the particular brand of music that was popular at the time. Unfortunately, it would seem that our own era will be remembered as the time in which those who could work a particular programme on a computer well enough to tune their voices into sounding nigh-acceptable were lauded as heroes, but that's neither here nor there. Anybody who complains that music these days is entirely awful just needs to dig a little deeper and, more importantly, accept that not everybody thinks the same way about it.

When it comes down to it, musical taste should never be a measurement of someone's value.

Some people like rock whilst others will listen exclusively to metal, and this doesn't make either of them less of an interesting or worthwhile person. Crucifying someone because they're a fan of Justin Bieber is pointless and short-sighted. The guy may not press all of your buttons, you may even think he's a talentless hack, but once again it's important to respect the beliefs of others. As it happens, I see more ad hominem attacks in the name of Bieber support (if you're reading, Justin, I apologise for using you as an example so often. Simplicity's sake, right?) than I do against him, but the concept is the same. It's imperative not to overreact when it comes down to something as superficial as musical taste, and it's very unbecoming to flare up just because one of your friends doesn't share your love for all things 'Vanilla Ice'.

Personally, I've found different music fits different occasions. This may seem obvious, but it's amazing how few people accept that all sorts of music can be effective and appropriate in the right instances. At parties, for example, dance music is inevitable. Instead of sloping sullenly into another room to avoid the dross that's coming out of the speakers, embrace it. Enjoy yourself, even if you don't enjoy the music. I've never liked it as a genre myself, but in certain situations it can really enhance the experience you have. In contrast, on quiet nights in I like to settle down with a nice jazz mix or slow acoustic sounds. Not everyone's a fan of either of those things, but why does that matter? I've whiled away many an hour listening to tracks other people would (and have, in my presence) called utter rubbish, but that never bothered me and shouldn't anyone else. Music is such a subjective pleasure that to judge anybody else on his/her tastes is frivolous and inane.

On my travels I've met people who absolutely love hip-hop, and more than a few who hated the mere mention of it. Pop can be similarly divisive, as can something like heavy metal. Everybody knows a few people who like it, and a few more who say that it's just noise. A close friend of mine is a heavy metal fan who manages to turn his music tastes into a joke at his own expense. After a while, people stopped caring about what he listened to and left him to it: his unflappable, self-depreciating humour became the perfect defence mechanism. In the end everybody has their own opinion, and me saying that I don't like something won't make anybody else like it any less. Having your own opinion is so important and a message that I keep coming back to, so if you genuinely enjoy someone that the masses have condemned and have a great time listening to them then all well and good. I'm voicing my opinion in saying that I don't, but feel free to turn it up all the louder if you truly enjoy it.

Music brings people together. I've spent many a happy hour trading songs with my friends, male and female alike. I find it's a topic that consistently remains interesting no matter who you're talking to, as long as the other person is open-minded. Realising you and a friend have a mutual affection for a particular band or style can be exhilarating, and it's always nice to have somebody to accompany you to concerts or festivals who you know will be enjoying themselves the entire time. In my experience, such occasions are wonderful opportunities to bond with someone and, while they're expensive, you'll never get a better gift for someone than a ticket to see their favourite band in the flesh. I've found that, almost invariably, live music eclipses listening via CD or any other means (yes, I'm old fashioned, and the proud owner of a CD player and blossoming disc collection) as the atmosphere of the occasion electrifies your experience of the music. I'd even go as far as claiming that I'd probably enjoy seeing good ol' Justin Biebs live on stage. Okay, maybe I'm pushing it.

In terms of playing a musical instrument, I'm told it can be extremely rewarding and infuriatingly taxing in almost equal measures. As a grade 3 recorder specialist (and proud of it) I am clearly in no position to talk on such matters, but a few of my close friends have significant talents in this field, and have huge chunks of their time eaten up by their instrument. On this particular musical aspect, therefore, I shall say only this. As with all hobbies, put as much time into it as you feel is necessary for you. Don't let your parents fill your heads with stories of never making it as a virtuoso pianist if you know in your heart that you never wanted to be one anyway. If you have fun with it, then by all means play the cello (or whatever) to your heart's content, but don't neglect work for it. Unless music really is your life's passion, you shouldn't be devoting huge segments of every day to it. It could be a relief from work, in which case you strum away like your life depends on it. For me, music is like a shoe collection. Some of your footwear fits certain occasions, and nobody will berate you for wearing your comfy slippers around the house. At the same time, everybody likes to throw on a nice pair to go out in, and going to the beach or heading out for a run requires further alterations to your lower wardrobe. Don't spend all day in the same pair of shoes, or they'll start to smell, and don't wear shoes that are shoddily made, or fall apart at the seams if you take away the autotune.

Chapter 17: RELATIONSHIPS

'Treasure your relationships, not your possessions'

– Anthony J. D'Angelo

Guys, you knew this was coming. At some point or another in the life of your average teenager, relationships and the emotional extremes that accompany them begin to occupy every waking thought, ceaselessly running through their (our!) minds like Usain Bolt after fifty cans of Red Bull. In terms of my own life, I think it's safe to say that a fair percentage of my teenage years have been devoted to the pursuit of a happy, healthy relationship, something which nowadays seems all-too-uncommon. In a world where a distorted 'reality' is all-too-evident on our TV screens and the mating strategies of the general population seem to be based around status and money rather than any factor that actually matters, like affection, shared interests or even (whisper it) love.

It's important for me to mention that I am not the best consultant for relationships, as they seem to exist today. I am not wholly experienced in every instance of today's relationship paradigm, but I feel well-versed enough to offer a reasonably comprehensive account of the best way to ensure that future relationships you may enter into are (at the very least) healthy and exciting, and to avoid stagnation and frustration as often as humanly possible. To start with, I feel justified in demolishing a few commonly held misconceptions surrounding courtship, starting with something I hear bandied around on an almost daily basis, that is the idea of 'leagues'. When it comes down to it, humans as a species are not entirely petty and small-minded, and for most sensible people good looks will not be the determining factor in deciding whether or not to pursue a potential mate. I will concede that in the embryonic stages of relationships sexual attraction does matter, and if you're not attracted to someone then it's quite unlikely that a relationship will work in the first place. Where the misconception comes into play is the definition of 'attractive'.

Unsurprisingly, there are no universally accepted criteria for what particular features make somebody attractive, and it's perfectly possible for two people of the same age and sexual orientation to look at somebody and see them with hugely different levels of attraction. I have experienced affection for people whom my friends have assured me are not in the least bit attractive, sexually or otherwise, to them. It seems that more often than not there is at least some overlap in terms of who is seen as attractive, but I feel my point still stands that beauty really is in the eye of the beholder. Besides, I can't help but feel that people often find a certain type of woman attractive due to the perpetuation of a lack of machismo by TV shows and films. In essence, we find attractive what we are told to find attractive. When it comes to the initiation of a relationship, one point to explicitly remember above all others is that whilst the opinions of your friends do and should matter when it comes to some aspects of a relationship, in terms of who is and isn't attractive the views of others should have no bearings on your own. You know who you like and it doesn't matter if nobody else finds them attractive. Nobody else is going to spend as much of their time with them. I've already spoken comprehensively on the sexual side of relationships but as an aside in this context, it's a whole lot more fun having an intimate relationship with someone that you find attractive rather than someone your friends have consistently assured you is good-looking but simply doesn't push your buttons.

A particularly cynical but nonetheless important piece of advice concerning relationships is to never let yourself get blinded because of how hard you've fallen for a particular person. On many an occasion I've witnessed the downfall of my (usually male, sorry chaps) friends who've become overly attached to their significant other and forgotten all about the people that really matter to them in the process. It's all too easy to fall into such a trap and plunge all of your time and energy into a single person, particularly if you aren't experienced on the relationship front. Frankly, this isn't helping anybody. The object of your affection will feel stifled and will no doubt push you away (this may sound unrealistic, but nobody appreciates full on affection all the time.) You can convince yourself you enjoy the intimacy for a while, but after that it just becomes a chore to even talk to someone you feel so inhibited by) whilst your friends won't take kindly to being treated so nonchalantly in the 'blossoming' stages of your relationship. As for you, you're left with an unhealthy partnership and a bunch of friends in a huff. So, how do you dodge this pitfall?

Well, to start with it's imperative that you maintain a grip on reality. The world doesn't stop turning just because you've entered into a relationship; everything doesn't change and you don't (or shouldn't) become a different person because of it. Be sure to remember who you are and never to let anybody change you, something that is particularly problematic when it comes to relationship. Be strong: Everyone is more open to changing when they're doing so for someone they love, but when it comes down to it the same rules apply, and there is no benefit to be reaped from becoming someone you aren't just to please somebody else. Keep your expectations realistic, and do the right thing for yourself. Be reasonable with someone you love, and never expect too much from them.

Don't get angry with someone because they've been with other people before you, because when it comes down to it that's water under the bridge and should remain that way. A fact that many people forget is that just because your lover has been in a relationship before it doesn't mean they aren't committed to your own, and it definitely doesn't mean they love you any less because of it. Some people lust after pure virgins due to some pathetic animal instinct that tells them that any girl who's been 'tainted' by somebody else is not fit for them to date. To put it frankly, this opinion is severely outdated and anybody who ascribes to it needs a serious reality check. If someone loves you don't waste your time debating with yourself about whether or not they'll go crawling back to their ex-boyfriend/girlfriend because they're a lot more likely to do so if you spend all your time thinking about meaningless past occurrences rather than the present and future. Love someone in the here and now, care about them and do things for them but never forget your friends and family, and above all remember who you are.

Chapter 18: HONESTY

'In a word, to appear an honest man it is necessary to be one'

– Boileau

Every lie only ever leads to another lie. It's the snowball effect in the most devastating way possible and I don't believe it's hyperbolic to say that lies escalate so quickly and mutate so grotesquely that it simply isn't worth telling them. Sure, they allow an easy passageway through many a tumultuous situation, but it isn't worth the reward. Besides, nothing worth having ever came easy anyway. Being honest as much as humanly possible is generally a good idea. Of course, exceptions arise, and I can see smug readers at this very moment mentally enquiring whether I would be so quick to defend brutal honesty were a violent axe-man to come a-knocking at my door, weapon in hand, and ask me politely the whereabouts of my family, who I happen to know are hidden away inside. Any sane person would surely dismiss the murderer somehow rather than invite him in to slaughter away to his heart's content. Dramatic situations aside, however, I am a firm believer in truthfulness. Honest.

It's always tempting to lie in certain situations. When someone asks you to come out and you simply don't feel up to it for whatever reason, the pull of the fictional familial responsibility can be inviting. I wouldn't begrudge anyone who considered this option, but I believe that barring a legitimate reason for denying the aforementioned invitation, it's in everyone's best interests that you, albeit with a moderate grumble as you resignedly put on your coat, take your friend up on this invitation. They didn't have to ask, and turning down offer after offer just makes you out to be the type who's never up for a good time, someone who would rather stay at home where it's warm than venture out into reality. Eventually, the same friends won't consider your company a valid option anymore, and the invitations will dry up. I've mentioned already that I'm all for a quiet night in with a nice book every now and then, but if it reaches the point where life has become little more than an endless cycle of work or school followed by an evening at home with little change on the weekends, something's gone wrong. Take people up on their invitations, and don't spend time concocting elaborate excuses should such a situation arise and you're unwilling to leave the cave.

Incidentally, it's amazing the amount of strain and effort people are prepared to put into their lies when the very reason they find themselves building them in the first place is to avoid just that. I've heard some beautifully elaborate fibs spouted which seem to have endless layers to them, so much so that the inquisitor usually gets tired of asking and leaves the person alone. However, every now and then an inviter simply won't take no for an answer, and continuously pokes and prods at the lie until it unravels. Here is where the nadir of dishonesty lies, when you find yourself having to invent on the spot, and remember it all for the next time someone asks you why you failed to attend the party / gathering/baby shower/ annual boat race/strip club opening/Greek play rehearsal (delete as appropriate) and implores you not to miss the next one. It's hugely draining to have to keep up a façade for an extended period of time. Far be it for me to call lying on the whole reprehensible; all I'm saying is that in my view it isn't a good idea. Socially, morally, spiritually, being dishonest can be damaging.

Earning a reputation as a liar is a bad thing to happen to anybody. Trust is so important in all walks of life and a label like that won't fade easily or atrophy over time. On the flipside of that coin (which I imagine as very much resembling the silver dollar belonging to Two-Face of 'Batman' fame: the liar's side gnarled and blackened and the honest side a glittering, spotless surface. Just a thought, and probably excessive, but I like my metaphors,) anyone who establishes a reputation as an honest person who shoots from the hip is likely to earn a lot more respect than they otherwise would on account of their attitude. Being the social creatures that we are, humans are drawn to someone that they can confide in and receive honest opinions from.

Over time, honesty becomes second nature. Practice something enough and soon enough it gets incorporated into your personality. If there's a single trait I can recommend alongside altruism, then it has to be truthfulness and honesty. Contained within this package is frankness, and avoiding telling someone the truth whilst not explicitly telling an untruth is no honesty at all. Telling somebody what they want to hear, bending the truth to fit a certain situation or outright holding back what your own opinion is when somebody requests it of you aids neither yourself nor the person who so eagerly craves support for the most part. In terms of white lies or tactless truths, the opposite is true. If attending the funeral of a horrible man, it might make sense to lie about his good character in order to keep his remaining relatives happy. If lies become a regular thing, however, these people will never stand on their own two feet if the only way they can feel good about themselves is through others showering them with ill-deserved compliments. Stick to your guns with people, and when they fish for compliments, maybe they'll catch a boot instead. Your words may be cold and rubbery, but they're real. And sometimes a reality check is all these people need to stir them from their stupor and set them straight on the path towards becoming a better person.

I'd much rather someone told me to my face how they felt about me and answered honestly when I asked them something. Sure, it'll sting coming out of their mouths, but it really isn't vitriolic for the most part. That being said, learning to toe the line between honesty and straight-up tactlessness is a key facet of growing up. Children unleash ill-chosen words with reckless abandon; adults pick their phrases carefully (as they should in all walks of life. I swear, readers, I won't stop beating this particular horse until all and sundry clean up their verbal act) whilst maintaining a firm grip on the conversation. It isn't difficult, and it's respectful as much as anything.

More than anything I'd advise being honest with yourself. Spending the weekends locked away with nothing but a few high scores to show for your hours alone is no life at all, and all to many people manage to convince themselves that they're achieving something, on the cusp of something, or will achieve tomorrow. Here's a tip from someone who's been in that place: nothing will change unless you take a long, hard look in the mirror and let yourself know that this isn't what you planned out. Be the one who soaks the sad sap in the reflection with a healthy dose of reality, and change for the better. It's not easy to be frank, to be that honest person, but it's something vitally important to do.

Chapter 19: ADVERSITY

'The wind in one's face makes one wise' –
Proverb

It's become clear to me over the past few years that it isn't easy being different. I don't mean to say that it's impossible; just difficult. People do treat you unlike everybody else, because when it comes down to it you are. It's a very human trait to be frightened by something unfamiliar, and in this day and age this subconscious fear is only ever exaggerated. As a result, it's imperative that if you plan to implement any of these processes laid out over these pages into your life that it is understood what you'll take the risk of facing: more than your fair share of adversity. I'm not trying to say that separating from the herd won't make you happy, just that it's a long slog sometimes and requires some serious grit and effort. People are often tempted to ascribe to a mob mentality in situations such as these, and for some reason or another I've noticed that people like me are shunned, either finding themselves radically unsituated within their little society (if they're unlucky) or a sort of 'social butterfly', flitting between groups. Whether this is entirely down to the aforementioned ostracising actions of the majority or the natural tendency of the minority to spread themselves rather widely I can't say. All I can say is that it's the choice to live as a wolf rather than a sheep, the price of which, according to Hugh McLeod, is loneliness. At least we'll stave off the boredom the flock is unfortunately stuck with.

A large part of learning to handle such an (arguably) lofty status involves learning to deal with being alone. It's a scary thought in every sense of the word, but it's a fact of life that every now and then you'll have to face an isolated existence. The priority has already been mentioned, which is developing enough hobbies to ensure that time isn't spent simply twiddling your thumbs in the absence of anyone to motivate you to do anything else. If you aren't careful, it's all-too-easy to fall into the trap of day after day of lying in bed, wondering about what it would be like to be like everybody else. I've been there, and it's awful. I think it's in inevitable portal to go through to reach what you want, a poorly constructed bridge that must be traversed to reach the other side, but that doesn't make it any easier. Sleepless night after sleepless night will take its toll on the hardiest individual and the ceaseless questioning never seems to stop. You'll wonder why the world is this way, what you're doing wrong, when it's all going to sort itself out, and how. All I can say is that it's temporary. People grow out of cliques and into themselves, and the future is so much brighter than the present seems to be. Holding onto hope takes you so far in this life, and I know that from a fair amount of personal experience.

Finding something to focus on means you'll never get sucked into this vortex of self-loathing, and never suffer from the equally damaging self-pity. It means you'll learn to appreciate (and even look forward to) time by yourself. There's the threat of becoming *too* isolated, but this is avoidable. Spending a balanced amount of time alone and with friends is the best route to go down, as it allows you freedom to express yourself with like-minded people along with enough hours to recharge your batteries with some well-earned alone time. It sounds weird to say that I spend a lot of my spare time thinking. I am able to formulate opinions and viewpoints this way by examining the day's events and seeing what led to what. This in turn means that I have a working knowledge of social situations themselves, which leads to the comforting realisation that solitary pursuit can be every bit as valuable as a day or night spent with friends. I feel that learning to enjoy your own company is of optimal importance as without a sense of self-appreciation (that, I must stipulate, is *not* the same as vanity or arrogance) an over-reliance on the company of your friends is an inevitability, which I have found leads to the degeneration of the oh-so-vital sense of self.

Having said that, I am sure that personality plays a key role in how one deals with lonesomeness and adversity. Some people manage to fit seamlessly into the role of outcast whilst others really struggle to be happy without a supporting cast of friends behind them. I do not aim to change those who prefer the company of others, but only to ensure that they do not become overly reliant on anybody but themselves. Whilst it is true that some friends last for a lifetime, they are few and far between. The one person who will always be present in your life, whether you like it or not, is yourself, so learn to deal with that fact.

What I said earlier about the niggling feeling that the world is built wrong being more or less temporary rests on those few penultimate words: 'more or less'. I still have existential crises every now and then when some fresh social Hell crawls out of the woodwork and I feel I have no way to combat it. There is always going to be another norm that you don't understand or agree with. I'm not saying you have to get on board with all of them; the key in this instance is tolerance. There are a lot of pastimes that have become integrated into society that aren't my thing, and so I must face a certain amount of stick for my reluctance to partake. How you respond to this is what matters, and it is so much better to maintain your principles and learn how to be alone than sacrifice them for the sake of group integration. Recall the story of my unfortunate acquaintance back in Chapter Three who couldn't bear the thought of being alone, and sold out in the worst way.

Sleep is a great healer. This might seem out of place in this chapter, but I've often found that those moments where the loneliness becomes a little too much can be quashed by a good night's sleep. It's refreshing, and if nothing else it's a few hours away from a world you don't understand, and one that doesn't understand you. A temporary solution to an on-going problem it may be, but an effective one nonetheless. The value of those mattress minutes shouldn't be underestimated or scoffed at. Next time you really feel like kicking off about an aspect of society you can't or won't understand, sleep on it. Things always feel better in the morning. In time, it becomes easier to accept that other people won't always agree with you or think the same way that you do. Reaching the point where you're happy just to be your own person and let the hate of others wash over you is a huge step towards constant contentment.

Chapter 20: GOSSIP

'Gossip is the opiate of the oppressed'

– Erica Jong

Gossip goes by many names. Rumours, word on the street, chit-chat. I utilise gossip because in an almost onomatopoeic sense I think it fully encapsulates what the word itself references: the flapping of lips for the sole purpose of spreading information that more often than not is private and irrelevant to the 'gossiper' themselves. This flapping sounds almost like the manic gobbling of a chicken, which is an apt comparison when you consider the fact that most people who do the gossiping are complete and utter wastrels (a certain pun employing a male chicken might have made sense here, but it seemed a little crass.) It always struck me as totally laughable that people exist who genuinely have nothing better to do with their time than discuss the personal business of others, and pass judgement. On that point, what gives the gossiper authority to decree what is and isn't acceptable behaviour? Surely the beauty of morality is that it is entirely subjective, meaning that what may be completely abhorrent to one party could underscore the entire belief system of another. This, however, is a double-edged sword, and means plenty of people can't wait to cry 'tolerance!' the minute somebody questions their hateful slander. Having said that, I can't quite comprehend how people can be so blinded by their own prejudices and unwilling (or, perhaps, unable) to grasp that others might see things a little differently to themselves.

It might appear as though I'm campaigning for an impossible dream, and to some extent that's true. At a basic level, 99.99% of people talk about others behind their back at certain points during their lives. What we have to remember here is that there's a huge difference between conveying an opinion and metaphorically pouring water on the beliefs of others. The passion with which I have heard some people pass judgement on those they consider to be their friends is staggering, and to me that's quite amusing. It seems that life would be a whole lot easier if everyone was a little more reticent to discuss business that wasn't his/her own, but that's easier said than done.

I would guess that one of the main reasons why people feel the need to gossip is that it's difficult for them to think about their own lives. Assessing the lives of others is a whole lot easier than assessing your own, but it's imperative that everybody learns to look in the mirror before they call others names. It seems that with all the bells and whistles adorning their metaphorical living rooms the general population has forgotten that their houses are made of some pretty fragile glass.

I'm not saying hold grudges forever, nor am I saying you should tell everyone what you think of him or her straight to their face. The former leads to passive aggression, the second to you being, for lack of a better term, a pillock. What I can advise is a little bit of unconventional therapy: talk to an inanimate object. I've recently been in a situation where I've had plenty to say with regards to the behaviour of other people, and somebody (or something) has definitely had an earful. The difference is, I'm directing my ire at the pages of a book. Time after time I sing the praises of writing down your problems because it's the best method I've found for releasing the emotions you sorely want to be rid of without hurting somebody else's feelings. All things considered, it's the best alternative to unfairly chastising somebody for a lifestyle choice you simply don't understand or agree with. You don't have to keep it, in fact it's probably better not to for risk of somebody finding it, but just the action of writing it will make you feel better.

Having said that, I've already mentioned how important it is to be honest with people, and not to hide behind expressed opinions that aren't your own for fear of offending somebody. Everybody in this world appreciates the truth, and you shouldn't be afraid of warding somebody off a path that's bad for him or her. Here, however, I must include a warning: there is a *very* thin line between expressing your opinion to somebody and viciously undermining theirs. To tread this line is to be a conversational wizard, and I'm not sure I know anybody who has mastered this particular tightrope just yet. All I can say is that it's important to remember your honesty as and when it is asked for, because as much as people want you to tell them what they want to hear, the truth will more often than not leave them in a better position. Don't offer your opinions unless the time is right and they're warranted by the conversation. You might hate drinking, for example, but it isn't your place to stop others from doing it, nor is it your place to berate others for it behind their backs. Keep your opinions to yourself unless they are specifically asked for.

In terms of being the gossipee rather than the gossiper, in the frankest way possible the only option is to deal with it. Understand that no matter how well you toe the line and present yourself as the very card and calendar of conversation, there's always going to be people that just can't help themselves from gossiping about you behind your back. You could be the closest thing to flawless and people would still find reason enough to scorn your life choices. The only way of dealing with this without resorting to a childish, underhanded back-and-forth with the gossiper in question is to accept that not everybody thinks the way you do, and that people will gossip even if you don't. I've had more than my share of 'discussion' but taking offense only ever exacerbates the situation. Much better to take it all as water off a duck's back, and coolly and calmly keep your head held high.

More than anything else gossip acts as a defence mechanism, and once you take it for just that you start to look at people in a whole different way. Those who are quickest to berate others often have the fleshiest underbellies themselves, if you'll excuse the contrived metaphor. Their slings and arrows can only ever harden you up to future assault though, so take each insult or shard of gossip with good grace. The fact that someone feels threatened enough to gossip about you strikes me as something to be simply laughed off, rather than be bothered by. Accept gossip as the only outlet for somebody's envy and it all becomes all the more amusing. Turn a sticky situation into a laughing matter and you'll be a whole lot happier.

Chapter 21: TRAVEL

'What singular emotions fill their bosoms who have been induced to roam!'

– Byron

Travel broadens the mind. As something of a whippersnapper myself (believe it or not) I haven't had the time to travel as much as I'd like but my brief foray into life beyond my own shores has shown me so many new things to love about the world. Having visited a baker's dozen or so of countries ranging from Canada to Oman I feel reasonably qualified to sing the praises of long-distance travel. I've spent hours on end aboard planes and trains and seen the sights and for that I am very thankful. I'm incredibly fortunate to have had the chance to see as much of the world as I have, and am blessed with a parent who adores the pure concept of travel and always pushed us into it at every opportunity. Although it might not always be exactly what you want to do, travelling is worth the time and expense ten times over. Seeing the world definitely opens your eyes and there's something about scrambling up a rocky mountainside to peer over the precipice of a magnificent oceanic vista that the (admittedly charming) hills and valleys of England just can't equal.

Imagine being born with monochrome vision. Life in your home country is purely black and white (for simplicity's sake, the metaphor allows for any colour), with no scope for expansion. Of course, you don't know any different, so it's not like you feel you're missing out on anything. Life is, and always has been, pretty grey. You wake up and throw apart your grey and grey polka dot curtains to let the glorious grey rays into your bedroom. You gaze out the window. 'My', you might think, 'isn't the sky grey today?'

Eventually the time comes to take a holiday. You could be eight years old or twenty-eight. The moment you step into a brave new world a brilliant colour fills your vision and you see things in a fantastic light that you've never seen before. The shades of black and white melt into awesome technicolour as your entire universe takes on a new hue. The sky is brighter, the snow is whiter, the grains of sand on the beach feel lighter. Having experienced this once, you'll long for it again. Travel is one of those bugs that you just can't shake, no matter how hard you try. The buzz remains the same time after time and each new filter reveals an entirely different vista of experience. Imagine an iridescent world that only gets more spectacular as you travel, a world that's more exciting and fluorescent with each country you enter, a world that has so many fascinating things to offer to anybody willing to experience them. That's what travelling does to you. That's why people spend billions every year on exotic holidays because once you go astray, there's no option but to stay away.

Not only does travel broaden your palette in a mental sense, it also allows for expansion in many other fields of experience. I could (and will) write an entire chapter about the weird and wonderful foods I've sampled, and you have my word that the opportunity to consume mountains of foreign delicacies is one that everyone should embrace with open arms. It's always depressing for your taste buds to adapt to the veritable smorgasbord of delights on offer only to return to the comparatively dreary doldrums of home, where fish and chips rapidly lose their appeal when placed alongside such impressive competitors. Don't get me wrong, I like the food at home as much as the next guy, but I can't begin to explain the sense of joy that some foreign culinary masterpieces have evoked in me, and no amount of good old British marmalade can smother those memories.

Quite apart from oral pleasures, the world beyond offers up the chance to experience different people. I cannot stress enough the importance of gaining acquaintances with a thoroughly different background and upbringing to your own. Granted, many people faced with this proposition will surely remind me that there is more differentiation between countrymen than there is between those brought up beyond one's own borders, but I insist that there is much more to be learned from interactions with the latter. Underneath the prejudices and class divisions everyone from a single nation has something in common. It's expressly difficult to pin down exactly what that is, but I maintain that this bond exists. With people of a different nation, there's so much more to learn. New ways of looking at and interpreting the world, new ways of understanding your surroundings, and even new ways of looking at the people closest to you. I've learnt more from a few choice conversations with people I've happened to meet on my travels than I have from extensive chatter with those who are blinded by their cultural upbringing, and can only view things from a single point of view. It's so exciting for me to hear stories of distant lands from those who have experienced them first-hand, and I always feel enriched for the conversation. There are so many shackles to be shaken off through travel, I can't emphasise that enough. Free your mind.

Travel also brings with it memories that will last a lifetime. Visions of hulking skylines, magnificent natural monoliths, and staggering monuments will stick with me until the day I die, and I've barely even begun my life. Sunset always seems all the more spectacular when it occurs over the craggy peaks of a mountain, and quite apart from anything else it's all so damn inspiring. I first started writing abroad because travel gives me so many different emotions that need releasing, in a way that nothing at home can. Travel is unique in that it allows you a means of getting away from the stressors of your home life whilst accelerating emotional progress ten times over. I've grown up a lot overseas, and some of the greatest memories I possess first arose far away from home. I have a lot to thank travel for because it was essentially the push that gave me the impetus to write in the first place. Now, as a secure eighteen year-old who will write whenever the opportunity arises, I am no less thankful for the wonderful springboard that travel proved to be.

Chapter 22: FOOD

'I'm at the age where food has taken the place of sex in my life. In fact, I've just had a mirror put over my kitchen table'

– Rodney Dangerfield

I, like most people, have a difficult relationship with food. At the best of times it can make my toes curl and leave me craving more. Sometimes I find myself drooling over it. It affects me in ways nothing else can and leaves me feeling satiated and satisfied... for a while. Of course, our relationship isn't quite as perfect as it might seem to the outside world. Every time we see each other I feel a certain sadness, like I've done something wrong. I find myself courting foodstuffs that I don't even like, simply because society dictates what's best for me. I think that with food, as with relationships, everything is best in moderation.

I've never been one to see the appeal of dieting. There's a lot more to life than limiting your food intake to a few measly salads a day, in my (cook) book that's nothing but a recipe for disaster. You'll only end up shovelling more food down your throat later to compensate, and that's not helping anyone. I see dieting as the wrong means to the right end. Sure, it might help you lose a little weight, but the endorphins you'll miss out on due to chocolate, sweets and all manner of wonderful things being cut from your palette means it really isn't worth the effort if you've been raised on greens. The psychology of dieting is really interesting though, and some people simply can't restrain themselves enough. Maybe completely cutting out the calories is the best choice for these people. However, far from simply cutting out the good stuff and wallowing in celery-based unhappiness, I recommend a compromise. Now, I'm as lazy as can be when it comes to some walks of life. You'll never find me jogging if I can help it, and the idea of lifting weights makes me wince. One thing that people who know me well will attest to is that I loathe the concept of caring more about one's physical appearance than mental capacity. Nevertheless, I have had the misfortune of experiencing life as an out-of-shape layabout and it's a status I never want to readopt. Everything is more difficult when you're unfit. Most readers will understand the uncomfortable sensation of carrying a backpack that might weigh only ten or fifteen kilos for a number of hours.

Imagine having to carry that around on your body, day after day. It sounds to me like something definitely worth avoiding.

So, we've established that stuffing your face, whilst infinitely pleasing in the short term, is a bad idea once you consider the potential ramifications. However, I'm not ready to surrender the savoury goodness of a hearty meal along with the sugar-filled forbidden fruit that is a delicious desert just yet, so I feel a compromise is in order. Luckily, Mother Nature has pulled through once again with a fantastic alternative to eating rabbit food for breakfast, lunch, and dinner. A little exercise is all it takes to allow you some leeway in terms of dieting. I've mentioned earlier how adverse I am to traditional exercise, but making it an enjoyable experience means you're a lot more likely to partake more often. For me, a game of football isn't about the exertion, though I can feel the sweat pouring off me at times. It's about the spirit of the game and the fun you have playing it. Exercise is, for me, an afterthought, but it's one that shouldn't be so quickly cast aside. I feel as though this advice can be applied to both genders, but I certainly know more guys than girls who enjoy a quick kickabout (with a few notable exceptions.) It does seem as though dieting and food are different ballgames for women and that there are gender differences when approaching the issue. As a boy I obviously can't say for sure what it's like to be a girl who needs to drop a few pounds, but exercise is vital no matter what you're packing down there.

In terms of balance, I've always been sceptical about the whole 'food pyramid'. I'm not saying 'pyramid' isn't an accurate word (the whole thing reeks of a government setup to raise the price of fruit and veg), but all I'm saying is I know plenty of people who eat close to a piece of fruit a week with no side-effects. I know parents the world over will condemn me for this, but I wouldn't pay too much attention to numbers on the side of boxes, preceded by an E or not. Anybody with a shred of common sense knows that you've got to eat a certain amount of everything to stay healthy, and limit yourself to a couple of splurges a week, which I think sounds very fair. None of this calorie counting lark for me, it always seems so petty looking from the outside in. There's a point where a healthy interest in something, like keeping in good shape, becomes an obsession, and that's cutting things a little fine if you ask me.

In terms of money, I'd recommend not worrying about it too much. I know too many people who refuse to buy anything that isn't top of the range, but I'd like to think readers of this book would have the good sense to realise that a bargain without a brand name can be superior to the overpriced oligarch of the food sector. Of course, when it comes to the issue of meat this all gets turned on its head. There is a significant difference between free-range meat and the processed, cheaper stuff which could fill a book on its own. I can't begin to describe the range and depth of the vegetarianism debate in such a short chapter, but like so much of my message it's entirely dependent on who you are. All I'll say here is that ethical considerations can and should play a role in deciding what you eat, but I won't condemn anyone for either being or not being a vegetarian or vegan. Either way, pay attention to what you're buying. If you're going to be cheap, more often than not you'll end up scraping (sometimes literally, depending on how frugal you really are) the bottom of the barrel. When it comes to food, I tend to lean towards quality over quantity. It's all well and good picking up several litres of a rancid juice drink for a few pennies rather than a better tasting, pricier alternative, but in terms of health you're probably better off taking the latter.

I can't begin to speak for anyone other than myself when it comes to intake. I have witnessed first-hand that everyone eats different amounts and until you sit down for a meal with somebody there's no way of knowing what that'll be. It's recipe roulette going out to dinner with someone for the first time, and I've found myself marvelling at people's physique to food intake ratio. I won't even pretend to be anything but a below-par mathematician, but something there doesn't add up. Nevertheless, I've come to terms with this anomaly, and accepted the fact that some lucky people can eat to their heart's content and stay skinny as a rake. For all you readers muttering obscenities under your breath at this point, I'm right there with you. For the other half of readers who sit with a smug smile on their face admiring their enviable physique in the mirror as they peruse this volume, go and grab another cake. I'm sure it won't do you any lasting damage.

Chapter 23: PATRIOTISM

'True patriotism is of no party'

- Smollett

There's an age-old debate surrounding the rationality of patriotism. One side claims that since we don't choose where we're born having pride in one's nation is nonsensical. The other accepts this but maintains that a certain level of patriotism is entirely acceptable, laudable even. It seems to me that it's all very dependent on the situation we find ourselves in. For some the government represents little more than an unshakeable anchor that will continue to weigh down the good ship UK (or whatever country they find themselves in) and stall progress. Therefore, such people struggle to be proud of a nation they disagree with on fundamental issues. Personally, though I've never been entirely on board with the system currently in place, I've always been a patriotic person who loves his country.

I can only speak from the position of an Englishman, but I suppose that's part of the point.

Everybody views things differently because, as I said a couple of chapters ago, a different upbringing inevitably results in a completely different attitude towards issues of government, national pride and the like. And since that's what makes life so interesting, I feel as though we should be proud of our roots. What matters is that I have my own story which is important to me, though it might not be to anyone else. Heritage is for me inexorably linked to patriotism, and it always interests me to think of the 'land of my fathers' in days gone by, and how different the world is now.

Patriotism is, strictly speaking, a love of one's country. Think about a man who loves his garden. He works tirelessly to cultivate it and keep it clean and tidy. Whilst this can't be extrapolated and applied to one hundred per cent of a country's inner workings, I feel as though it's an apt comparison. It's true, however, that our gardener could turn rogue and begin to harness his 'love' of his plot into something more malevolent, and begin to use this to justify evil actions (perhaps he'd use those garden shears for more than just hedge-trimming?) towards other gardens. This can be compared to a country justifying warfare on the grounds of patriotism, but that's an extreme case.

I feel as though I'd much rather live in an Eden of our own creation than a dank hovel, strewn with weeds and laced with despair. Some might argue that it's stupid to like somebody more because they're geographically closer to you than somebody else, but that isn't what I'm arguing. I'm merely suggesting that we make the best of the place we find ourselves in and learn to love our surroundings as best we can.

Patriotism can drive people to do great things. I've recently witnessed my country host what was, by all accounts, a staggeringly grand Olympic games. There was raw passion aplenty and it wasn't just the athletes that showed such drive; everybody even remotely involved with the whole process was magnificent, because we as a country were determined to put on one hell of a good show, and we delivered. It's moments like these that back up my claim that patriotism is no bad thing. I witnessed first-hand what people can do when they unite under a common aim and strive to build something together. I can't help but think that without that urge to 'make our country proud' we could never have achieved anything like the success we did with the Olympics. The royal family might not be everyone's cup of tea, but in terms of world-renowned iconography there's no denying that they're up there with the Statue of Liberty and Ayer's rock.

Things change constantly and the world (and the microcosm of each country) changes with them. Governments are born and die but each country lives on. In time I'm sure England will be vastly different to the way it is now. Nevertheless, I know that we'll still have choirboys belting out the verses of 'God save the Queen' with all the energy of their Victorian ancestors. The country continues to renew itself and it's remarkable to me that though the founders of each nation are now long dead, the peoples of today still commit to much the same values that they held eons ago. I relish the traditions that have survived over the centuries and happily sit down to chow down on my fish and chips like every true Englishman should. Having said that, whilst it's respectable, laudable even, to love one's country, in my opinion it's all the more important to recognise our similarities over our differences. I realise that I've said a lot this chapter about loving one's country, but there's a great difference between love of country and holding on to traditions that are quite clearly outdated and irrelevant to a modern world. Just because I enjoy the strains of 'God Save the Queen' and love football as much as the next man doesn't mean I can't see that the country is in constant flux. It is bound to change with every passing second, but I see nothing wrong with grasping harmless but charming traditions and keeping them alive and fresh. I know that feeling too strongly about one's country can lead to violence and negativity, but I believe that patriotism isn't the same as xenophobia or jingoism. For me patriotism means recognising that somebody adores their own country just as much as you love yours, and living and letting live. We all live in the same world, but that's not to say that we shouldn't love our own little plot of land.

Chapter 24: CHANGE

'Nothing was born. Nothing will die. All things will change'

– Tennyson

As the boys of Keane once crooned, "Everybody's changing, and I don't feel the same". Like it or not, in a weird paradoxical sense change is here to stay. It happens throughout our lives but never more rapidly or terrifyingly than in our teenage years. I, like so many before me, experienced the upsides and downsides of the adolescent white-water and am a better person having survived such a turbulent existence. I find myself now as a strong, confident young adult and the world is my oyster because I'm capable of being myself. However, I'd be one hell of a liar if I said I hadn't experienced significant change in the run up to these halcyon days I find myself enjoying now.

One dramatic manifestation of change, particularly in young people, is physical development. For some readers this will no longer be relevant, but many of you will be embroiled in the insufferable period of one's life in which various body parts grow and shrink, expand and contract, and even change colour. In order to maintain some air of class about this text I'll simply say that change happens to everyone and puberty smiles on some more than others. I'd begin to sound like a broken record if I said that looks aren't the be-all and end-all one more time, but it's the truth. 'Leagues' in the colloquial sense of the word don't exist, at least not on a physical basis, so don't waste your time worrying about how the opposite sex is going to perceive you when your face is covered in acne/grease/braces/who knows what. It's a larval stage of humanity that everyone has to go through, and you've got to deal with being an ugly caterpillar before you're able to spread your wings as a butterfly.

Change on a mental level is much more significant regarding the rest of your life. A change in attitude is essential as you venture through adolescence, and it's all-too obvious when somebody has a child's mind in an adult's body. Being a grown-up is easy once you understand that the challenge is in the name: to be a grown-up means growing up and not just physically. Being a twenty-three year old 6'4 beefcake with no social skills isn't being an adult, it's being a man-child. The times are constantly changing, and if you want to be taken seriously in life you'll change with them. There's nothing worse than somebody who's stuck as a child all their life unable to take the leap to adulthood.

Other people will change. As you age and time passes you'll lose some people who are close to you. Situations will change, you'll move about, and sometimes those special friends that you thought would be there forever drift away like an ice floe from the glacier. It's a natural process and there's no point dwelling over a lost friendship. By all means, fight like a dog to keep your friends close if you can envisage the companionship you share with them being maintained (via mutual input and a lot of TLC from both parties) for the future, but if it just isn't working then sometimes you have to let people go. It's scary but it happens. I've lost people who I never thought I would because, when it comes down to it, that's life. The friends I have now aren't replacements for the one's I've lost; they're just the next step on the staircase.

Change is always going to be unpredictable. That's the beauty of it, and it's also what makes it so frustrating. You'll never be able to plan ahead in life, because things change with every minor decision. Something that has always astonished me is the extent to which apparently insignificant choices can impact on the future in massive ways. I often look back at the past year or so of my life and think about how different things could have been if I'd said something different, or acted in another way. Once you admit that change is a part of life it all starts to feel a lot more natural. Embrace the uncertainty of life, because it's all a massive adventure. What happens in your final chapter is undecided, and it'll stay that way until you get there.

I guess that underneath it all we really do rely on change to keep our lives interesting, and to motivate us to wake up each morning. I'd much rather exist in a world that shook me around and kept me on my toes with both highs and lows than one that left me in a constant state of neutrality. Life is wild, and accepting that is part of it. Look back at the past and see how much has altered for you in the past year. If it's a lot, then fantastic. That means you're on the right lines, and can hold your head high as you turn it towards the brightest of futures. If nothing's changed, then go out and make it. Don't accept a mediocre routine when you could be getting so much more out of life. A real man or woman should exist in a constant state of flux. Nobody's perfect, so once you stop critiquing yourself and streamlining who you are, slowly chipping away at flaws, you stagnate. Be the person that lives to change and changes to love. Be proud of who you've made yourself into, and be willing to adapt as a person outside the herd.

Chapter 25: UNFAIRNESS

'Unjust rule never endures perpetually'

- Seneca

Don't be naïve. Life is bound to throw some rocks in your path no matter what field you choose to excel in, and you should be aware of that from the start. Apologies for such a grim start to the chapter, but sometimes you need a "shake-'em-to-wake-'em" sentence or two to remind people of the harsh realities that the world has to offer up to us, on a plate that's bound to shatter into a million tiny pieces, each one sharper and more painful than the last.

To be honest, failure is sometimes pretty much inevitable. Barring an incredible run of good luck, nobody reading this (hell, nobody at all) is going to coast through life without ever encountering injustice. In the face of adversity, the exploits that matter aren't those that you achieve unencumbered, they're the feats you manage to perform after you've dragged yourself from the very doldrums of unfairness. The most exceptional moments in life come from snatching victory from the jaws of defeat, greatness from the cusp of obscurity. If it came down to me, every human being would come hard-wired with a certain tenacity, an indescribable vim and vigour which spurred them to keep coming at a problem until they simply couldn't go any more. That in itself is the essence of my message here - accept that things will go badly a lot of the time, and the times when things go smoothly will be all the more appreciated as a result.

This is one of those times when an example really helps the issue at hand. If you'll forgive me, readers, it's time to get a little dark. I am by no means after any sympathy here, so I have no plans to turn this into a pitiful lamentation. Nevertheless, we've all had a little hardship in our lives, and I don't know a single person that hasn't had to contend with some mighty misfortune in their time.

Right now, I'm in the midst of a maelstrom of familial illness. Relatives I've grown immensely close to are getting sicker by the day, and there's nothing anybody can do about it. These people mean so much to me, and I'd do anything to see them recover… but I can't. It's a horrible situation to be in, but it's one that we all need to accept.

Pulling our weight is hardly enough help to anybody, but it's the best we can do. Short of committing every waking hour to fundraising, which would subsequently be plunged into every research centre in operation, we're stuck keeping our heads up, and our hearts strong. I've learnt over the course of the last few years that while it's okay to cry, the flow's got to stop sometimes.

Like I said before, this isn't a story about how I learned from my tears as a boy to become a hardened and mature adult. It's a story about the child that lives inside all of us, and the importance of checking up on them on a regular basis. There's only one way to deal with the inevitable hardship we face as a species, and that's to vent. Everybody has a different way of expressing their exasperation and frustration that life doesn't always go to plan and those that don't tend to realise that they should get one pretty sharpish. Whether it's reading, writing, or even just talking through your problems with somebody else, acceptance is the final phase of more than just grief.

It's going to be hard sometimes. Every now and then life hits you like a ton of bricks and it's almost impossible not to crumble in a heap.

What's of primary importance is knocking yourself back into shape, rather than reforming to accommodate the problem. I'm not saying life shouldn't change you, but to allow your entire personality to shift on the back of an unfortunate event is only going to make things worse in the long run. Softening the blow is a nice thought at the time, but allowing yourself to alter and change by not facing up to your issues is, more often than not, something that'll hang over your head, because it's a hell of a lot harder to change forwards than to change back.

It is often hard to move forward without understanding, or at least some form of closure. Mystery breeds malcontent. We've all been there; the aftermath of a disastrous event and the only question that springs to mind is 'why?' The truth is, there usually won't be an answer. This doesn't mean settle for dissatisfaction, instead it means that sometimes you have to dig a little deeper. More often than not the answer's not something tangible or easily grasped. You really have to wrap your head around some problems to even begin to understand them or why they happened in the first place. If there's still nothing coming then I have some uncomfortable news for you: there might not be anything there. Life has a knack of kicking you while you're down, and sometimes it all comes down to plain bad luck. In those cases, you're almost forced into acceptance by default. No signs of a direct source of the issue means nothing to dwell upon, even if you wanted to, and perhaps that's for the best in itself.

Embrace the emotion that comes with misfortune, but avoid traps and pitfalls. It's a moment of misery followed by a new beginning, and we should treat it as such. Toil and hardship isn't something we should be lamenting, it's a chance to show the world just how tough we are; a chance to show everybody that we're not ready to lie down just yet. Take the chaff with the wheat, the lows with the highs, the frowns with the smiles, and never let life get the better of you. It's going to be unfair from start to finish, so be ready to deal with that.

Chapter 26: DEATH

'Thou know'st 'tis common, all that live must die, passing through nature to eternity'

- Shakespeare

Death is one of those things that you know shouldn't bother you, simply because it doesn't make sense to. Instead of lamenting the fact that somebody's gone, we should be rejoicing in the time we got to spend with them in the first place, recalling blissful memories and beautiful happenings of yesterday. Unfortunately, in real life things aren't so simple. Try as we might, we can't assuage the negative emotions surrounding death. It is, and always will be, the end of a life, and that's a concept hard to accept. The thought that we'll never share experiences like the ones we had with the dearly departed invariably outweighs the recollection of those already enjoyed, and in a world where change is ubiquitous and the passing of time is unstoppable, death is, and always will be, the one true constant. Sometimes that's a hard truth that people refuse to grasp, but it's one that all of us will face at some point in our lives. I can't explain the processes of death or why it happens, only that it will. And boy, does it hurt. More often than not we break down and cry like children.

And with good reason. It matters not that crying is a sensible way of releasing our emotions: in this scenario, healthy living goes straight to the back burner. What matters is that remembering, lamenting, feeling on such a level is what makes us human. The overwhelming flood of emotions that only death can bring is as beautiful as it is saddening. To see a mother cry over her son doesn't just pull at the heartstrings, it frays them. It is the briefest of windows into the pinnacle of human emotion; pure melancholy, unsullied by any bias or social expectancy. When we cry we show our souls to the world and open up the deepest, darkest parts of ourselves for all to see. In a strange way death reveals our true faces.

People beg and pray that they'll never have to deal with death, at least not in compromising circumstances. I say that these people deny themselves an essential component of life. When they shut their eyes to the end, they miss what made the beginning and the middle so special. We need death to remind us just how brilliant life is. Death isn't pretty and it never, ever gets any easier to face it. Those who fear it are only those who feel they don't truly deserve it.

To some a long life is a curse. They wish to greet death sooner than others, eager to meet that which has touched every human, every tree, everything that ever lived. To those we should not preach. Their choices are their own, and they know better than anyone when their time has come. "Now more than ever seems it rich to die." These words of Keats resonate as much today as they ever did. Just as an expectant mother knows intuitively when the time for labour is near, death comes to most not as a surprise but right on time. Ever-punctual but occasionally abruptly early, death tends not to play games with us. He hardly has the time for that.

Chapter 27: BRAVERY

'True valour lies halfway between cowardice and rashness'

– Cervantes

Courage is the life blood of the best of us. It is as relevant now as it was in the days of Shakespearian heroes and heroines, and binds us to the great adventurers and warriors of history. To be a truly monumental human being requires huge courage and great commitment to a cause, a commitment that must remain staunchly unshaken in the face of great adversity.

Bravery doesn't mean doing something stupid, or even something that you're scared of doing. To me, exhibiting courage means keeping your head in situations where everybody else would be losing theirs, as Kipling might have said. A brave person is one who is able to not only acquit him or herself in the face of adversity, but someone who does it with poise and a clear head. Someone with an itchy trigger finger who, by a stroke of luck, manages to take out an evil dictator is not brave, but someone who sits down with his or her parents and slowly and deliberately outlines their lifestyle choices is. Bravery is all about nerve and not adrenaline.

Perhaps you would call someone who jumps from the highest diving board 'brave'. It seems to me that the English language is (once again!) limited here, and doesn't include a word for this particular branch of bravery. Bold or simply risky go some way towards describing what I mean, but don't quite get there. Recklessness doesn't fit so for the sake of brevity I'll call that type of bravery 'daring'. It's possible to be brave without being daring. I've known plenty of people who wouldn't dream of going toe to toe with any insect bigger than a gnat, but are still some of the bravest souls I've ever met.

Being brave does not mean putting up with something undesirable. In fact, to me it means the exact opposite. Being brave means showing real mettle in the face of bad blood, and fighting for something you care about in a careful, calm but nonetheless resolute manner. Standing up to a teacher who says something sexist is bravery; standing up to your parents when they do something stupid is bravery; most importantly of all, standing up to your friends is true bravery. A spat with someone you barely know isn't courage, but stating your opinion to your friends when they try to lecture you is.

I spoke in an earlier chapter about peer pressure and how important it is to not get sucked in by the expectancies of your friends and indeed wider society. The onset of peer pressure can, however, be a great opportunity to exhibit bravery, and thereby advance as a person. In the face of huge pressure, being brave and strong enough to go against the flow is an achievement indeed. Mockery and ridicule may come, but those who stay strong despite popular opposition – and do so with good grace - are truly the brave amongst us.

Bravery goes hand-in-hand with self-confidence. If you can force yourself through toil and hardship and go against every human instinct to conform, then your confidence will skyrocket. The feeling of knowing that you stood your ground, and took action for what was right even when every sinew of you was stretched towards what was wrong never gets old, never stops being exciting. Whether it's acting in the knowledge that punishment will be forthcoming or simply doing what is right despite the threat of isolation or unhappiness, being brave takes a certain kind of individual. An individual who can bounce back from adversity is rare indeed. If you can become one of them then fear and hesitation fall at your feet. To be truly brave is to fear nothing.

To be courageous is to be true to oneself. In the midst of fear and uncertainty this is exceedingly difficult. The temptation to stray into the slow lane (where everybody else has set up shop) is massive. Bravery, however, is not exhibited by a single act of self-respect but by a constant maintenance and upkeep of honesty to oneself. In this way bravery becomes not an action, but a habit. By endlessly supporting oneself and sticking to your guns whilst the world around you crumbles into a faceless mass of regularity, you become brave by default. Granted, such a lifestyle is tiring, exhausting even, but is worth the eventual reward. Self-confidence, wisdom and peace are the prizes for putting yourself through the original difficulties of bravery. It may seem like I'm exaggerating when I say that bravery is one of the key constituents of a happy life, but I'm not. Being brave means ripping off your shackles and feeling the breeze on your naked body, open to the elements. If you aren't yourself, then you won't ever be truly happy, as a life filled with imitation and disguise is exhausting to the point of unhappiness. Being brave means being happy.

Chapter 28: SACRIFICE

'Was anything real ever gained without sacrifice of some kind?'

– Sir A. Helps

Sacrifice, more than anything else I've mentioned thus far in this book, goes hand in hand with maturity. It takes a special kind of person to consistently put others before themselves, and another being entirely to do so when it means the loss of their personal wellbeing. In evolutionary terms, it's hard to place the life of anybody that isn't our own child before our own, but I would argue that bridging the gap between the care you offer to yourself and that which you offer to others is one of the most adult things you can possibly do, and will stand you in good stead indeed as you circumnavigate the tumultuous waters of adulthood. Sacrifice involves a great deal of grit and it can be difficult to understand at times.

Personally, I've always found it hard to wrap my head around sacrifice. It always seems like the right thing to do, and yet I feel horrible every time

I do it. I'm quite ashamed to admit that nine times out of ten, going out of my way to help someone has left me embittered and rueful. "Could not that money/time/physical labour", I ask myself, "Have been better spent on something to make my life easier?" Following that, of course, comes the inevitable flood of accompanying guilt as I assure myself that putting down whatever was occupying my attention at the time and doing something for somebody else is worthwhile, even if I do a terrible job of it. After all, it's the thought that counts.

But is it? I've always been of the persuasion that when it comes down to it it's action that really plays the starring role. If I actively give up my valuable time (I could've been playing Rollercoaster Tycoon!) to benefit somebody other than myself, then surely that's a better option than 'my thoughts are with you' or any amount of sympathetic chatter (although, staying up into the wee hours just to talk to somebody who's having a hard time could definitely be classed as sacrifice) you may muster. In my eyes, to work for others is to improve yourself. You'll begin to feel much less miserly, which in turn leads to actual, tangible generosity, without the searing mental pangs of guilt or injustice that come at the begin. Ironically, putting in a little work into placing others before yourself diminishes the negative feelings sacrifice originally brings on. You become a better person through learning to enjoy giving aid and help others at the same time, all without feeling a shred of uncertainty or reticence about it. What's not to love?

So what's the lesson here? Put everyone before yourself, always? That's being a doormat, and whilst it may help others, it's showing enormous disrespect to yourself. Sacrifice means missing the concert you really wanted to go to so that you can attend your friend's birthday party. It doesn't mean countless hours spent writing embarrassingly terrible poetry to a girl that wouldn't even bat an eyelid were she to read it. I've been there, and whilst you're certainly risking your own enjoyment (constantly getting your hopes up when you know deep down they're only ever going to be dashed isn't that much fun, surprisingly), there's no version of this where you're helping anyone else. In fact, you'd probably help the poor girl and yourself a little more if you just dropped the act and told her how you felt, or simply resolved it yourself and moved on. This isn't a story for this particular chapter, but it felt relevant. It's vital to realise that sacrifice is not a case of doing things for people that don't want or need your help. It's when you're there for someone in need whether or not it's completely out of line with every plan you'd made, and you're there ready and willing to put yourself on the line.

Without trying to talk too much about sacrifice as if it were a Biblical ritual, I must say that it brings us mutually closer together. It seems that the age-old phrase - 'what goes around comes around' is once again proved correct in the case of sacrifice, as the more you give up to help other people, the more you'll eventually gain through charitable means. It's a beautiful circle, as minimal outlay results in the more income than you could possibly imagine. Sounds like a pretty damn fine business venture to me, so why not invest? Put yourself to the test, and try your best to help one person a day, whether or not they deserve it. It doesn't matter. Lay your cards out on the table, and expose the parts of you that are vulnerable. Sooner or later, your true friends will pay you back. And it won't just be for 'a favour', or 'a solid'. The people that really matter will help you at their own expense because they know you'll cover for them. Make yourself into someone that deserves that level of sacrifice and life will be so much better as a result. Furthermore, people will begin to see you for what you have become – a warm, sunny, positive person.

Chapter 29: CONVERSATION

'Better a witty fool than a foolish wit'

- Shakespeare

And so, finally, we arrive at a chapter on conversation. Be honest, you knew it was coming as soon as you picked up this book and flipped through the first couple of pages. Conversational wizardry is something often coveted but seldom possessed, and those that master the art of chatter are truly revered (and rightly so) amongst other men. Being handy with a snappy comeback or a quick witticism is a very useful thing in this life, and to improve my conversation is a daily aim. It's a skill, but at its best it approaches an art form. The to and fro of a challenging argument; the tension of a heated debate - I'm too excited. What goes into a fine speaker is the same as what goes into a truly fabulous footballer. Poise, class, precision and more than a little razzle-dazzle.

Just to be counterintuitive, I'll start with the very best speakers, la crème de la crème, the ultimate in dialogue and discourse. We all know at least one, and they're bloody intimidating. Able to seamlessly slot into any conversation without alienating anybody or seeming like they don't fit, these are the true captains of confabulation. The ability to engage with something you are otherwise ignorant about and probably not interested in is undervalued these days, and every CEO in the world is looking for someone who can carry a conversation on their back. The world leaders are (almost) always big talkers, and when they aren't, it shows. Some infamous leaders of our time are more noted as blabbermouths than politicians, and never help themselves by the flapping of their lips. The true key to opening the doors the world sets in front of us, be they labelled 'business', 'social', or even 'self-confidence', is a good grasp of what it takes to chit-chat. Everyone remembers Martin Luther King because of how magnificent a speaker he was, getting his message across in the best way possible. Words have so much power in today's world, and nowadays the conversationalist is the alpha human. Most important of all is the ability to maintain interest with vim, vigour, and speed of rebuttal. Imagine someone who carries around a dictionary with them at all times. Whenever they speak, they must look up the perfect word for the task at hand, and subsequently read it out in a slow, monotonous voice. This person might strike us as a pretty shoddy conversationalist. That's because to be interesting and engaging you need more than just the words. You need the subject matter, the energy and, most importantly, the interest of your own.

There are shortcuts to achieving affable conversation skills even if you're a naturally shy person. Be excitable and engaging, and don't let your flame be diminished by the fact that you really don't care. It isn't being dishonest to take interest in something that's never grasped your attention before; it just means you're adult enough to branch out. You'll learn something from whoever's busy telling you about their dust collection or hand-built matchstick unicycle. Not to say that those things aren't particularly interesting, but they have a reputation as such and therefore make for good examples. People flock towards those who can be entertaining and interesting at the drop of a hat, and stay for the sheer wealth of information those people have to offer.

Humour is a vital constituent of good conversation, but there's a time and a place. Fortunately, the times and places where humour isn't appropriate (at least on some level) are few and far between. Even at a hospital, some light comic relief is often appropriate, or even required. Having the sharp wit and ability to read a conversation to know the perfect moment to insert the perfect joke is a gift, but it can be cultivated in us lesser mortals too. It sounds absurdly simple, but take each conversation as it comes, and greet each with happiness. Don't be afraid to be made the fool, and make jokes at your own expense over mocking others. Good conversation should be a back and forth sparring session rather than a one-sided barrage of insults and petty 'jokes'. In good grace, the light-hearted jabs at oneself are the ingredients for fine conversation. This shouldn't change when it comes to speaking with the opposite sex, though it all-too-often does. All rules go out the window when people begin to speak to someone they're attracted to, and it's often uncomfortable to watch.

I find it fascinating that in this, the conversation that evolution should surely by now have isolated as THE vital constituent of the modern mating ritual, all tact and sophistication vanishes, making way for sleazy double-entendre to take its place. Men and women alike boast their way through conversations not dissimilar to those encountered on the playground, with pulling girls' pigtails replaced by undermining their confidence through 'clever' backhanded compliments and suchlike. It's endlessly amusing, mainly due to the fact that none of it really works. If all you want is a quick hook-up then sure, act in such a way, but don't expect anything concrete to emerge from such petty beginnings. Instead, treat the opposite gender as people. Converse with them, rather than talking at them. Discuss rather than deter. Above all, have something more interesting to say than 'I really like your shirt'. You're not fooling anyone, pal, we all know you're only interested in what's underneath.

Chapter 30: SLOWING DOWN

'I'm a slow walker, but I never walk back' –
Abraham Lincoln

Every day that goes by, things speed up. Cars, trains, boats, planes, the internet, the telephone, the bullets in the combat zone. Technology is evolving at a hell of a speed, and we are being dragged along with it. We're hurtling down the rabbit hole and things are only getting darker. Childhood passes in the blink of an eye nowadays and it's a childhood unlike any before it, mine included. We zip through our teenage years and bam, adulthood, in all its gruesome glory, jumps our bones. We cascade through life on a freight train, none of us with the ability to really dig our heels in, shudder to a grinding halt and take in our surroundings. What's the rush?

I'm scared about turning twenty-one. Hell, I'm scared about turning nineteen. The thought of adulthood and responsibility terrifies me. The worst part is there's no avoiding it. Try as we might, age takes us all, and even my devilish good looks will fade with time. Nevertheless, I'm more or less prepared to take the frightening leap across the precipice because I've experienced so much in my life thus far. I feel that despite my fears and faults, I've learned enough to be a notable, well-adjusted nineteen-year-old. I have the same emotion every birthday, because I try my very hardest to live each day in my life in as exciting a way as I can. I know that you reading this can relate to the feeling that we can't slow down the flow of time any more than we can stop it altogether, but we can slow down our lives. There's something to take away from every day, no matter how dismal it may seem at first, so it's important to be positive.

Embrace life. Fall in love with as many aspects of it as you can, with a sombre nod to those depressingly unavoidable facets. When there's hardship, think about how much more you'll appreciate the good times. Be sure to make each day count, and take each evening to look back on the day's accomplishments and plan for those to come tomorrow. If you get your act together, they'll be plentiful. People so rarely take the time to revel in their health, and they only really miss it once it's not there anymore. I've witnessed first-hand what the deterioration of good health can do to somebody's state of mind, and it isn't pretty. There's a certain expression that walks hand-in-hand with the realisation that you've wasted so much of your life, and it's soul-destroying. To see the light in somebody's eyes slowly dim as they realise they've burnt themselves out before their time is something I never want to see in anybody else. But, more so even than that, I never want to see those eyes staring back at me in the mirror, dim like the scattered ashes of a dying fire. The light is there, but not for much longer, and we never realise how much we'll miss the heat until we're stuck out in the cold.

I'm not saying don't have 'lazy days'. It's always been my opinion that we need time off from the hustle and bustle of the working world to relax and recuperate. In fact, in order for my theory to stand up we need these days for reflection. If we obsess over filling each and every day with activity and progress, we'll never savour anything in life. It's akin to necking glass after glass of expensive fruit juice (humour me, I'm teetotal, remember?) without stopping.

Indulge in activities that you won't be able to again anytime soon. Don't feel that a relationship or a job is necessary at a young age. When you're a child, be a child, and don't be afraid to be. I realise that this lesson will probably come too late for most readers of this book, but I can encourage those still in their teenage years (and beyond, it's never too late!) to chill out, ease off and watch the world go by the way it was meant to be watched.

There's so much to love about the world, and especially our own unique journeys through it. People use 'you only live once' as a justification for crazy, outlandish antics, but I see it differently. To me, the fact that you only get one life means you should go as slowly as possible in it. Wring out every drop of life as an eighteen-year-old in the 365 days before your nineteenth, and so on as you journey through life. That way, the only end point I can envisage is one where I am exhausted, old and thoroughly ready to face death. Go slow, and savour the journey instead of always harkening after endpoints. In life, that's what really matters. Paint your own pathway with care and precision, and dust off your hands with a prideful sigh as you shut the door on a long life entirely lived.

Chapter 31: HOPE

'Hope! Of all ills that men endure, the only cheap and universal cure!'

– Cowley

Before I start this chapter proper I'd like to insert a disclaimer of sorts, an explanation of the content within it. This chapter on hope does not presuppose that hope can solve all problems and I'm certainly not naïve enough to suggest it can make us happy. It's a tool and an incredibly useful one at that. I believe that an ample supply of hope and a firm grip on reality can work together to give us the best outlook and sunniest disposition possible. One without the other doesn't work and you need to be able to realise when something's a lost cause, and entirely hopeless. Nevertheless, the power of hope should not be underestimated. Though Marx and others like him spoke at length on the damaging influence of a false consciousness, that's not the type of hope I'm referring to. I speak of the hope that allows us to stop crying and wipe the tears away from our faces, the hope that permits us to smile despite the hardship that weighs heavy on us. The hope that keeps us going.

We need hope to keep us grounded. Throughout our punishing teenage years, the light of hope remains unerringly bright. It might seem further away at times, but we know it's there. There are some amongst us for whom hope doesn't exist, those poor souls that descend into dark depression and sometimes never come out. One of my best friends found himself on that path and never got off. It was terrible to see his descent and it made me all the more determined to grab onto hope with both hands and never let go if I could help it. When things are easy we always hope that such blissful simplicity continues. When the going gets tough we hope that things will improve. I'd like to use this chapter as a tribute to that which has dragged me through the hardest of times, and helped so many others on their journey towards enlightenment.

I'd like to get quite personal now, and I hope that you'll forgive me for it. I used to hate the thought of the future - any future - living the life I did. The way I saw things, there wasn't much point in looking forwards. When the present doesn't make you happy, the thought of continuing in the same vein is painful, to say the least. It shocked and confused me to think that every time I applied myself to something, I had it thrown back in my face. I vividly remember an instance in junior school when we had to choose two people that we were sure we wanted in our class with us next year, a means for the school to keep friendship groups together. Of course, despite my best efforts, neither of the people I picked chose me. Acting the way I thought was right had never led to anything positive and I felt trapped in my own life. My self-respect plummeted as I realised once and for all that my lifestyle wasn't going to change itself any time soon. I was left a prisoner in my own distorted existence.

It was hope that released me from this sensation. Hope that I could do something for myself rather than for other people, and hope that those same people could accept my choice. Hope that I could push past the bonds of insecurity and fear to really change myself for the better. The encouragement of my family helped me to develop. It was their fond hope, that I shared, for me to make something of myself that drove me to start writing. I guess things haven't turned out too badly in that respect, and I exist today as somebody who still appreciates wholeheartedly what hope brought to my life. Without hope, I would still be coasting through a life that I wasn't enjoying, in the guise of somebody I wasn't. Hope, and not just my own, that I'd be able to completely alter my life gave me the power to do it.

As I've aged, my hope hasn't dwindled. A fire still burns within me, driving me onwards, keeping me motivated. If I didn't have hope that I'd be able to help people with this book, and that it would be appreciated by at least a few people, then I wouldn't be writing it in the first place. Ambition walks hand-in-hand with hope, and it's impossible to get far if you can't make both work in tandem. Whatever you're aiming towards, large or small, be sure to hold on to your dreams. Hope that things will change is no good without enough input to make those cogs turn in the first place, whilst ambition without hope leads only an early exit as soon as things get tough. It is as if ambition is the engine and hope the fuel that drives it. Nothing goes until both are in place.

Hope shouldn't dwindle with age. I've seen too many adults who've stopped relying on hope, and exist without goals or endpoints to reach. Sure, they might look on the bright side, but hope and optimism are very different kettles of fish. Critical thinking is required for hope to come into play, and without an active mind the optimism we might feel about the future is destined to stall. We need to harness hope to give us that extra push, one that all the good thinking and strategic planning won't.

It's fascinating to think how central hope is to the religions of today, and how important something so transcendent and incorporeal is to billions of people. All over the world people are putting their eggs into the baskets of their respective gods, crossing their fingers that they've picked the right guy. A strength and confidence stems from this religious hope, as people put absolutely all of their trust in their faith system. It is my argument that hope can do this for us all, in slightly different fashion. The thing about hope is that it doesn't have to help you put faith in anybody else; it helps you to believe in yourself.

I can and will accomplish what I want to. Hope that it's possible means formulating plans of action and routes to success is almost second nature. Hope means a happier existence too. Finding hope in our darkest days makes for focus in the lightest, and both direct us, firm and true, down the path to achieving everything we want. Mark Twain spoke of a 'Hope Tree' and prayed that it would never stop blossoming, and I would argue that it's all down to us. We'll get out what we put in from this life, and if we water our trees with vigour and ambition, we'll have a whole lot of hope, and a whole lot of happiness because of that.

Chapter 32: THE END

'When I stand before God at the end of my life, I would hope that I would not have a single bit of talent left, and could say, 'I used everything you gave me'

– Erma Bombeck

And so thirty-something chapters after a painfully adolescent opening introduced you to my take on things, the pages are beginning to run out. I can see readers shuffling about in their seats, glancing at the clock, drumming their fingers on the table. Don't fret; I won't keep you much longer. Funnily enough, after blabbing my way through tens of thousands of words across plenty of topics of discussion, I'm finally running out of things to say. The reason for this isn't laziness, or a lack of insight, it's the fact that in the end experience alone is what allows us to change. No author in the world can teach you how to be a better person, because it's a step you take unassisted. No more crutches, no more wheelchairs… it's time to step out of the support structure, and tentatively walk unaided down the path towards change.

Extend your reach as far as possible. Hopefully, I've helped you to recognise just how a big a bird you can be, and the worst possible course of action you could take now would be to settle for life in a small cage, content to grow to the size of your container, and no further. Feel that there's no quota on what you, I or anybody else can do, so don't let the world around you cast you a role you don't feel you're meant for.

The world isn't your oyster, but you can certainly shape your own life into something you really enjoy. It would be a travesty not to accept that, and worse still to think it a lie. Anybody can be spectacular these days, and with enough grit and determination there's nothing we as a species can't do. Let there be no limit to the vision of your mind's eye, and may you all achieve something wonderful in your lives before you kiss the world goodbye.

We're a species that's never finished, never adult, and even now we're barely reaching a juvenile stage. In a strange way we're simultaneously too old, too adult and too aged on account of modern medicine, but underneath the wrinkles we're still children at heart. Death is a reminder of our own mortality, and that scares us. I suggest that it shouldn't. For all of its power, death is not frightening, because it has to happen and makes me part of the legacy of human existence. Every great man and woman has died, and we are all a part of that, embers from the same fire. That day is nowhere near today, but I know it exists in my future. It isn't scary to think about, because try as I might, I won't live forever. I'll grow old and die. So will you, and your parents, and everyone you know. We'll become part of the faceless ocean that is humanity's history, and I think there's something beautiful in that. Enjoy this life to the fullest, treat others with the utmost respect, and warm yourself in every ray of sunlight you possibly can... you'll miss the warmth once death's cold embrace envelops you. Be passionate, brave, and love the ones that matter. In death, as in life, memories last forever, so make them worth remembering.

I feel like a parent prepping their child for the first day at school. It's as if I've given you your brand-new rucksack and crumpled sandwiches, and am trying desperately to say something meaningful to leave you with. Ultimately, this journey is yours. If my words can inspire you to change yourself, then wonderful, but I'm not deserving of credit. If I help one person then I'll be happy, content in the knowledge that it certainly wasn't a waste of my time. I hope you can break through the manacles of modern social pressures and turn yourself into a solid, well-adjusted, happy person. I may never meet you, but it's a privilege to have written for you. It is my fond hope that I've made a difference.

Harry Noad speaks to young people at schools up and down the country about how to be happy.

You can contact him anytime at

harry.noad@gmail.com

Printed in Great Britain
by Amazon.co.uk, Ltd.,
Marston Gate.